Red Roses and Petrol

In her home in Dublin, Moya is preparing for the funeral mass of her husband, Enda. From England and America, her children are returning for the sombre occasion. But as the ghosts of the Doyle family's past begin to materialise, the consequences are both profoundly disturbing and memorably comic.

Red Roses and Petrol was commissioned by Pigsback Theatre Company and premiered at the Project Arts Centre, Dublin, in May 1995. It transferred to the Tricycle Theatre, London, in July.

Joseph O'Connor was born in Dublin in 1963. He attended University College, Dublin, from 1981 to 1986, gaining a first-class honours BA in English and a first-class MA in Anglo-Irish literature. Thereafter, he attended Oxford University for a brief period before working for the British Nicaragua Solidarity Campaign. In 1988 he became a full-time writer. His works include several filmscripts; the novels, *Cowboys and Indians* (1991) and *Desperadoes* (1994); *True Believers*, an anthology of short stories (1991); *Even the Olives are Bleeding*, a biography of the Irish poet Charles Donnelly (1992) and *The Secret World of the Irish Male*, a collection of journalism (1994).

by the same author

fiction
Cowboys and Indians
Desperadoes
True Believers

non-fiction
Even the Olives are Bleeding
The Secret World of the Irish Male

Joseph O'Connor

Red Roses and Petrol

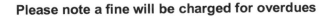

Methuen Drama **Modern Plays**

First published in Great Britain 1995
by Methuen Drama

ISBN 0–413–69990–0

A CIP catalogue record for this book
is available at the British Library

Typeset by Wilmaset Ltd, Birkenhead, Wirral
Printed by Cox & Wyman Ltd, Reading, Berks

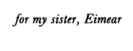

for my sister, Eimear

Red Roses and Petrol was first presented by Pigsback Theatre Company at the Project Arts Centre, Dublin, on 9 May 1995. It transferred to the Tricycle Theatre, London, on 11 July 1995. The cast was as follows:

Medbh	Kathy Downes
Moya	Anne Kent
Catherine/Young Moya	Deirdre O'Kane
Tom/Young Enda	Barry Barnes
Enda	John Kavanagh
Johnny	Paul Hickey

Director Jim Culleton
Set Designers Fiona Leech and Fiona Whelan
Costume Designer Marie Tierney
Lighting Designer Stephen McManus

Act One

Lights up on a cluttered living-room in a slightly battered suburban house. Two doors, one leading to a hallway, the other leading to the rest of the house. A window or two in the back wall, through which a night sky can be seen. A few visible tree branches suggest a garden.

The living-room contains a tatty three-piece suite which has seen better days. A man's overcoat, black, is draped over the sofa. There is a coffee table. There are three or four long trestle tables arranged around the room, with bowls of fruit, bottles of wine and beer, tall stacks of glasses, plates of sandwiches and delicatessen food covered in sheets of polythene and tinfoil. There are many funeral mass cards somewhere else in the room, possibly on a mantlepiece, or on the window-sill. But perhaps the most striking feature of the room is that it is full of books.

There are bookshelves absolutely groaning with thick academic books. More books lie in tall stacks around the room and on the window-sill. Books on the coffee table. An open suitcase full of books on the floor. There are several tea chests around the room and these, too, are half full of books. A large television in a corner with a video machine. As the play opens, the television begins loudly playing the Irish national anthem: the RTE 'closedown' sequence of rural scenery can be seen on the screen.

A middle-aged woman, **Moya,** *is kneeling on the floor, working her way through one of the piles of books. She is examining the titles of the books, throwing some into a tea chest and making a smaller stack of others. After a moment,* **Moya** *picks up the remote control device and lowers the volume of the national anthem. She stands, puts the remote control on top of the television, goes to the window. The national anthem is still playing, but more quietly.* **Moya** *looks out the window, then at her watch. She comes away from the window, looks at her watch again, begins to busy herself around the room. She arranges more dishes of food, more glasses, more bottles of beer and wine.*

Her daughter, **Medbh,** *a woman in her late twenties, wearing jeans and a jumper wanders into the room from the hallway and sits on the arm of the sofa. She is speaking on a cordless phone.*

Medbh   Stop! Don't say another word, you poxy wagon. I never said that.

Moya (*pantomiming shock*)   Medbh. Language please.

Medbh (*ignores her*)   I never said that, you dope. No. Who else was there? Yeah? That fellah's too stupid to brush the dandruff off his shagging Ray-Bans if you ask me . . . Yeah. And he'd fuck a frog if it stopped hopping for five seconds . . . It's true.

Medbh *stands and looks around herself for the remote control device. She cannot find it. She goes to the television, turns it off manually, thus silencing the national anthem. She then finds the remote control device on top of the television, picks it up, points it at her mother's back and presses, as though it is a Star Trek weapon.*

Moya *begins arranging a vase of flowers. She starts to softly sing the song 'The Leaving of Liverpool' while* **Medbh** *comes back to the sofa and sits down.*

Moya
So fare thee well my own true love
When I return united we shall be . . .

Medbh   If you wanted to I could. Yeah. The mass is eleven o'clock, and then the cemetery at half twelve. Are you coming back up afterwards? Ma'd love to see you. Well, she's . . . yeah. She's surviving. OK then, see you, petal.

Medbh *hangs up.*

Moya (*still singing softly*)
It's not the leaving of Liverpool that grieves me
But my darling when I think of thee . . .

Medbh   Mairead says hello.

Moya   Oh good, love. How is she?

Medbh   She's fine. She's got a new job.

Moya   Good.

She finishes arranging the vase of flowers.

There. What do you think?

Medbh She said she'd try and drop over tomorrow. She's not sure she'll be able to. But she'll try.

Moya *is unhappy with the flowers and begins arranging them again.*

Moya Good.

Medbh With her mother.

Moya That's good, love.

Medbh And Elvis.

Moya Good. (*She looks around the room.*) All done now.

Medbh Good.

Moya *looks at her watch.*

Moya Look at the time, love. It's time for bed for you.

Medbh I'm grand for a while, Ma. It's early enough yet. Do you want a cup of tea or something?

Moya *begins fiddling with the flowers again.*

Moya Or maybe put them all like that. Or inside in the kitchen. What do you think? Maybe on the stairs.

Medbh MA! Do you want a cup of tea?

Moya Haven't I been telling you for years? Don't call me Ma. I'm not a feckin' sheep.

Medbh Mother, mother, mother. A máthair. Mater. Mère.

Moya (*with some sarcasm*) Oh lovely. French.

Medbh I don't mean mère, French. I mean you're a dozy old mare, like a horse. Like they'd eat you in France. Or ride you, Mother.

Moya Oh, I've a lovely family all right.

Medbh (*in exaggerated Dublin accent*) Ah, sure God and all his holy saints bless us, but you do, Juno.

Moya (*laughs gently*) Don't start all that again.

Medbh (*continuing in O'Casey accent*)   Are you right there, Joxer?

Moya (*laughs and imitates* **Medbh***'s accent*)   I'm here, Cap'n. And ye're a daarlin' man altogether. Oh, a daaaarlin' man.

They laugh.

Moya   Terrible to be laughing. Would you not go on up though, love? Tomorrow'll be a long day you know.

Medbh   I was going to wait up for Catherine. Do you want me to make you a cup of something?

Moya   I don't know what I want tonight.

Medbh   Well, do you want a whiskey or something?

Moya *looks at her watch.*

Moya   I don't know where that sister of yours is. She should have been here at half past.

Medbh   It's foggy out at the airport. They were saying on the news.

Moya   Do you think we're after doing enough though? With the food? There'll be so many people.

Medbh   It looks lovely, Ma. Would you stop fussing around. You're giving me a headache.

Moya   Well, I just hope there's enough. It'd be terrible if we ran out. There's nothing worse than a funeral where they run out of food. It embarrasses people.

Medbh   We won't run out.

Moya   I don't know. People can eat a lot when they're upset. I remember at Uncle Liam's funeral they had one plate of sausage rolls between the whole lot of us. That's your Auntie Fidelma of course. She wouldn't spend Christmas, that one.

Medbh   How in the name of God would we run out?

Moya   Your poor father's the last of that whole family to go, you know. Not one left now, out of all those children. Imagine.

Medbh   I know, Ma.

Moya   Do you think our friend will come though, love? Do you think he'll change his mind?

Medbh   Don't ask me that, Ma. I don't know.

Moya   It'd be great now if he came over. Do you think he will, though, Medbh?

Medbh   I don't know.

Moya *goes to the table and rearranges flowers again. Suddenly she turns.*

Moya   But now, at a time like this. I mean, what did his father ever do to him that he wouldn't come?

Medbh   I haven't a clue, Ma. You know what he's bloody like.

Moya   Maybe if you gave him one more ring. He could come over in the morning, Medbh. Because they have the early flights from London now.

Medbh   No, Ma. He didn't get on with daddy, and that's not going to be changed now. So don't involve me, all right?

Moya   Your poor father. A man would think he'd be entitled to have his own children at his funeral, whatever else about it.

Moya *puts her hands to her face and begins to cry.* **Medbh** *goes to her and embraces her, sighing.*

Medbh   Don't, Ma.

Moya   Well, has he never heard of mercy in his life? Or compassion?

Medbh   Ma. Stop it. You know it always makes me feel pointless when you cry.

Moya   But I keep thinking, what went wrong with all of us?
As a family? What did we not do for you that we should
have done? . . . And to see the way things are now, when we
should all be together. Because it isn't right, Medbh.

Medbh   Ma, look, I know we're not exactly the Waltons, all
right? But we're not the Addams Family either.

Moya *smiles, in spite of herself.*

Medbh   Ah stop your cryin' now, Juno.

She caresses **Moya***'s face.*

And poor Missus Tancred now, and her son gev his young
life for Urland. Me daaaarlin' son, all riddled wit bullits.

Moya *laughs.* **Medbh** *points to the window.*

Medbh   Joxer, Joxer. What is the stars?

Moya *laughs again. She slaps* **Medbh** *playfully on the arm.*

Moya   Stop it you. You're terrible.

She pulls away from **Medbh***.*

They're lovely flowers they sent. From the university. One
from the library staff and one from the Arts faculty.

Medbh   Yeah.

Moya   And a lovely note from Professor Thompson. Did
you read it?

Medbh   I read it.

Moya   Your poor father. Such a lovely note from Professor
Thompson. He's such a lovely cultured man too. He always
sings Gilbert and Sullivan at parties.

Medbh   Dad always thought he was a smarmy old bollocks.

Moya   He did not, Medbh. That's an awful thing to say.

Medbh   He did. He said he never read a book in his life. He
said he was a culchie little chancer who plamased his way to
the top.

Moya   God, I never remember him saying that.

Medbh   He did all the same. He said he washed his suits in the washing machine.

Moya   He was always good to your father anyway. Enda never would have done as well in there if it wasn't for Professor Thompson.

Medbh   Ah rubbish, Ma.

Moya   It's true, you know. There wasn't too many from Usher's Quay had a job in the university library, I can tell you.

Medbh   Dad would have got on fine wherever he was.

Moya   Well, I'm not saying that. I know that. But he was good to Enda. And Catherine too, when he was her tutor in there.

Medbh   I remember sitting at the next table to Thompson once in the Belfield restaurant. And there was this young one with him, from Finland, with tits on her like she was deformed or something, and he was giving her the hairy eyeball, you know. And he says to her, well of course, Guy de Maupassant is my favourite author. And I thought, gee is certainly something that gobshite knows all about.

Moya   That's terrible, Medbh. That doesn't sound like him at all. Sure, he and Maureen are a lovely couple, considering Maureen's nerves. She'd take a bite out of a lightbulb, the same poor girl.

Medbh   Oh, it was him all right. Dirty looking eejit.

Moya   You stop spreading slander, Medbh Doyle. Now listen, come on and help me do a few more of these.

They both kneel, examine books and put them into tea chests.

Is Jerry coming back to the house tomorrow? Afterwards?

Medbh   Maybe. I don't know.

Moya   How do you mean, you don't know?

Medbh   I mean I don't know. Look, I may as well tell you, Mother, now you're not to go ballistic on me.

Moya   What?

Medbh   We split up on Sunday night.

Moya   Oh no, Medbh love. Why?

Medbh   Ah, he was getting on my nerves. You'd swear we were married for fifty years the way he went on at me.

Moya   But he's very fond of you, Medbh. Anybody can see that. You've that poor fellow wrapped around your finger.

Medbh   Well, he can be fond of someone else now, the big miserable bollocks.

Moya   You've a very hard streak in you, love. If you had a row or something . . .

Medbh   We didn't have a row, Mother. He was just . . . Ah, he wanted to be with me all the time, you know. Jesus, if I looked sideways at anyone else he'd nearly have a period about it. And we never went out with a crowd or anything, just him and me and his fucking ego and his oh Medbh, Medbh, I love you so much.

Moya   God, you poor dear thing. Some girls would love that.

Medbh   We went to Mairead's party a few weeks ago, and Charlie Foster was home from Australia . . .

Moya   Oh I see, said the blind man. I thought you'd a look on you when you came in that night.

Medbh   What do you mean a look?

Moya   I thought you had an expression. You and Charlie Foster were always thick as two thieves.

Medbh   Well, I hadn't seen him since he got back and we just had a bit of a dance, you know, and your man nearly chews the head off me on the way home in the taxi. Don't you humiliate me in front of my friends ever again, he says, in his Kerry bloody accent. Jesus, I nearly smacked the skinny face off him.

Moya   He's got the measure of you anyway. You're a terrible flirt.

Medbh   I am not. The cheek of him talking to me like that.

Moya   You've a gamey eye. I've seen you in action often enough.

Medbh   He was useless in the sack too.

Moya   Medbh!

Medbh   Well he was, Ma. Jesus, the original three-minute hero. You could boil an egg by him.

Moya   Stop!

Medbh   Do you know what he says to me one night? It'd help me, Medbh, if I could think about someone else, you know, when we're making love.

Moya   My God Almighty.

Medbh   Yeah. I said, that's fine, petal, it'll make a change from you thinking about your fucking self anyway.

Moya   You did not say that.

Medbh   I did. And I told him he had a sweaty arse.

Moya   Medbh Doyle, would you stop that talk. I'll have to send you down to confession if you keep on talking like that.

Medbh   Bless me, Father, for I have sinned, I'm after gropin' a fat sweaty arse. Do you know what Father Morton'd say, Mother? He'd say, oh, that's an awful sin now, love, for if it wasn't we'd all be doin' it.

Moya   Stop now.

Medbh   And they *are* doing it anyway, half of them.

Moya   You're lovely, you really are. Poor Father Morton isn't like that.

Medbh   Sure he's a *face* like an arse, Ma. Even Annie Murphy wouldn't do the bizz with Father Morton.

Moya *shakes her head. She looks at her watch. She stands and goes to the window.*

Moya   Where is that girl?

Medbh   She'll be here soon enough.

Moya   I suppose I'll go on up and just rest my eyes for a while, if you're going to stay up for Catherine. Maybe you'd give me a shout when she comes in.

Medbh   Yes, why don't you? I'll bring your tea up to you.

Moya *takes out a pack of cigarettes and lights one.*

Moya   Do you not think we should phone him again though?

Medbh   No I don't, woman. And why are you smoking that thing?

Moya   I just feel like the one. Don't be nagging me now.

Medbh   You'll give yourself cancer, you know. I'm worn out telling you. Or you'll have to have an artificial lung, like a big accordion, playing The Walls of shagging Limerick while you're breathing your last.

Medbh   God, Medbh, don't. And your poor father not even buried.

Medbh   He'd agree with me, you know. If he was here.

Moya   I hate to think of him down there in the church, all alone.

Medbh   I know, Ma. I know.

Moya *sits on the arm of the sofa and* **Medbh** *takes her hand.*

Moya   Because you know what your father was like. He never liked to be by himself. He often said that to me: 'You know, Moya, it's a terrible thing to be alone.' I remember this one time we were on holiday. Just after I lost the child.

It was when we went over to Majorca. And there was this woman on the tour, you see, and she was an awful bore. She was one of those women with pink hair and a tracksuit and a big necklace around her neck with her name printed on it. And everyone hated her, but your father kept asking her to come on day trips with us, you know, to different places. She was a middle-aged girl and we were still only a young couple really. She'd a terrible gra for the booze, good God, when I think, she'd suck the amontillado out of a dishcloth, the same poor girl. And she was well upholstered too. And she'd sing off-colour songs when she was tipsy. She was a fright now. And one night I said to him that I was fed up being with her. And putting up with her nonsense. And this terrible look came into his face. Of sadness you know. I'll never forget it. And he said to me, 'Moya, have you never heard of loneliness in your life?' God, I felt two inches tall then. I saw a really different side of him then, when he said that to me. Loneliness.

Medbh He'd a lot of different sides all right. There's some wonderful people in the world and daddy was definitely two of them.

Moya Don't now, Medbh. You know he was very fond of you.

Medbh I know he was.

Moya You know well what the problem was there.

Medbh What?

Moya You were too like him. That was the problem there.

Medbh God, I hate it when you say that. I'm not a bit like him.

Moya He'll never be dead while you're alive. You've the same wilful eyes anyhow. Look at you. You'd say night didn't follow day if you were let.

Medbh Well, it doesn't matter now anyway. Do you want that tea or not?

Moya I suppose so, yes.

Medbh *leaves.* **Moya** *rearranges plates of food and glasses. As she does this, she sings a snatch of a song.*

Moya
   . . . Now then Holland is a lovely land
   And on it grows fine grain
   It is a place of residence
   For the soldier to remain . . .

She kneels and begins sorting through a suitcase full of books. She removes some and finds a plastic bag underneath. She looks inside the bag and finds six or seven video tapes.

Medbh *enters with a tea tray.* **Moya** *continues examining the videos.* **Medbh** *puts the tray on a table.*

Medbh   Listen, I'm sorry, Ma.

Moya   For what?

Medbh   For what I said. About daddy.

Moya   What did you say?

Medbh   I thought I might have said something bad.

Moya   No. You're all right, love. It's a difficult time for us all, God knows.

Medbh *opens a can of beer for herself. She notices the videos.*

Medbh   What's on those?

Moya   I'm after finding them here in the case. I don't know what they are.

Medbh   Do you think they're dirty ones?

Moya *(tuts)*   Stop that. Give me another hand here.

Medbh *comes back to her mother and kneels down. They continue working, examining books and putting them into a tea chest.*

Medbh   The thing is, about daddy. He never forgave me for what happened with Luke.

Moya   Well, that's best forgotten now, darling.

Medbh   I know. But I wish we'd been able to make up about it. If he'd just once in his life said he saw it my way.

Moya He was set in his ways, love. It's great for kids now the way they're so open about everything.

Medbh But did you two really never do it before you got married?

Moya My God, are you joking me? There were times I wouldn't have minded, to tell you the truth. But he never even touched me until after we were married, that's the gospel truth. And we stayed virgins for a good while after that.

Medbh Really? They didn't hang the sheet out the hotel window the morning after the wedding?

Moya Indeed they did not. The only thing hanging out the window next morning was your Uncle Liam. No. It was six months before anything happened in that department.

Medbh Seriously?

Moya Well, I mean, we'd kiss, you know, and we'd hold each other. There would have been a lot of fondness there. And gentleness. But we were shy, I suppose. Sure, I never saw your father naked until after you were born. We'd make love with the lights off, you know.

Medbh Me and Jerry did it like that too, so I couldn't see how fat he was.

Moya Stop it, you rip. Anyway, I liked it like that, in a way. I thought it was more romantic in the dark.

Medbh Ma! You dirty heathen beast.

Moya Well, what? That's just the truth.

Medbh You big floozy, Mother.

Moya God, floozy indeed. When I think of the little we knew. But I loved the sound of his voice in the dark. And the little things he'd say to me.

Medbh Like what?

Moya Well, you don't think I'm going to tell you.

Medbh Ah go on, Ma.

Moya   Well, he'd call me little pet names. Oh, look at the holy innocent, you know well what I mean. He'd talk to me while we were . . .

Medbh   Moya, Moya. Undo the bleedin' handcuffs, willya.

Moya (*slaps her playfully*)   Stop it you. You're far too curious now, for your own good.

She stands. She picks up the coat from the sofa.

It's nearly a shame to throw away his old coat, isn't it? When he loved it so much. Maybe Johnny'd like it.

Medbh   Hang it up anyway. You don't want creases in it.

Moya *hangs the coat on a door.*

She kneels beside **Medbh** *again and they resume sorting books, putting them into a tea chest.*

Medbh   Complete Poems and Sermons of John Donne?

Moya   Yes. Poor Enda loved that one.

Medbh   Poetical Works of Percy Bysshe Shelley?

Moya   Yes. What class of a name for a man is *Bysshe*, do you think? Holy water was never poured on it anyway.

Noise in the hallway. Enter **Catherine**, *a woman in her late twenties.*

Catherine   Mum?

Moya   Catherine!

Catherine *throws her arms around* **Moya**. **Medbh** *comes to them. All three embrace, fighting back tears.* **Moya** *kisses them both.*

Moya   I didn't hear you coming in, love. How are you?

Catherine   I'm all right, Mum.

Enter a young, slightly-built man, **Tom**, *carrying two suitcases.*

Catherine   Oh Mum, this is Tom Ivers. He came over with me from New York. Tom, this is my mother.

Moya *is surprised to see* **Tom** *but hides her surprise. She composes herself and holds out her hand.* **Tom** *takes it.*

Moya I'm very pleased to meet you, love.

Tom Likewise. And I'm sorry about what happened, Mrs Doyle.

Moya Well, it's a terrible loss, Tom, for us and for a lot of people.

Tom I know. I mean it must be.

Moya Yes. For all his colleagues in the library. And all the students too. We've all lost something very precious.

Tom I'm sorry for all your trouble.

Catherine And Tom, this is my sister, Medbh.

Tom *and* **Medbh** *shake hands.*

Medbh Hi.

Tom How's it going?

Medbh Grand. Yourself?

Tom Sound as a hound.

Moya Well, there's tea in the pot. You must be famished.

Catherine No, I'm tired just. I ate a bit on the plane.

Moya Well, there's sandwiches and things. You'll have a sandwich maybe, in a little while.

Catherine I'm fine really. How are you, Mum?

Moya Oh well, I'm keeping busy anyway. I haven't had time to think much. There've been all the arrangements and everything, you know, but Father Morton has been very good, I must say.

Catherine I still can't believe it.

Moya No, pet. Well, look, you'll have a bite of something now. I'll just go and put the kettle on. Or would you like a drink maybe?

Catherine Maybe later.

Moya *helps* **Catherine** *out of her coat. She is wearing a fashionable and smartly-cut dress.*

Moya   God, look at the style. Turn around and give us a gander.

Catherine *turns.*

Moya   Oh, you look a treat, Catherine. It's lovely to see you looking so well, isn't it, Medbh?

Medbh   Yes, Ma.

Moya (*to* **Medbh**)   I wish you'd buy yourself a few clothes. You'd look lovely if you got yourself a few new things.

Medbh   Yes, Ma.

Moya   Amn't I lucky though, Tom? To have two lovely young women like these two?

Tom   You are.

Moya   You know, Tom, sometimes I think I'm the luckiest woman in Ireland.

Moya *leaves.*

Catherine   How is she?

Medbh (*with sarcasm*)   She's delighted. How do you think?

Catherine   I tried to get over sooner.

Medbh   Well, you're here now.

Catherine   So were you there? When it happened.

Medbh   Yeah.

Catherine   And?

Medbh   And what?

Catherine   Well, did he say anything? What?

Medbh   Catherine, the man was in a coma. He didn't say anything. They rang us up at five in the morning to say he wouldn't last and we better go down. So we drove down to

Vincent's and by the time we got there he was nearly gone. And we just went in and sat with him for a while, waiting for the priest. Ma held his hand. And he didn't wake up again.

Catherine   So he had nothing to say?

Medbh   Jesus, no. He had nothing to say, Catherine. He was too busy fucking dying, you know?

Catherine   All right all right.

Medbh   Christ Almighty, what do you want him to say? The Charge of the fucking Light Brigade or what?

Tom *snuffles with laughter.* **Catherine** *glares at him.*

Catherine   I just thought he might have said something. That's all. I just thought . . .

Medbh   Well he didn't.

Catherine   All right, he didn't. Forget it.

Medbh   You've been watching too much television.

Catherine   Christ. We're off already.

Tom   Should I wait outside or something?

Catherine   No no, you're fine. Stay there.

Tom   I feel like a stretch of the legs anyway. After the plane.

Medbh   You're all right, Tom. Sit down. I'm sorry.

Tom *sits down.*

Medbh (*to* **Catherine**)   I'm sorry, all right?

Catherine   It's OK. So. How are you?

Medbh   Tuesday was bad. I'm OK now.

Catherine   How was Mum?

Medbh   She was all right, I suppose, when it happened. I mean she knew it was going to happen, so . . . But then it was terrible seeing him. In the coffin, you know. She got a bit weepy then.

Catherine   Fuck.

Medbh   Yeah, fuck. And there was a big row down in
Vincent's because she wanted to wash him, you know, and
lay him out and everything. She told the nurse she did that
for her father and she wanted to do it for dad too.

Catherine   Jesus, really?

Medbh   Yeah, and they wouldn't let her. And when we
went down to see him then, it was awful. Because it sounds
stupid. But he looked like a dead person, you know? He
didn't look like dad. I didn't really recognise him to be
honest, the way . . . His hands looked so odd or something,
wrapped around the rosary beads. And they'd combed his
hair the wrong way. I mean, they'd combed it to the wrong
side, you know, across his head, to make him look like he
wasn't bald. He looked like Jackie fucking Charlton lying in
the coffin. It was terrible.

Catherine   I couldn't believe it when they rang me. I
actually . . . do you know, I actually thought it was a joke,
when they rang me in work. Some sort of sick joke. Isn't that
terrible? And then I got the number of the hospital. I made
them give it to me and I wrote it down, and I rang it straight
back. But the same woman picked up the phone and she said
no, it isn't a joke, love. I'm afraid it's true. Daddy's dead.

Catherine *almost lapses into tears.* **Medbh** *goes and hugs her.*

Catherine   No. I'm fine. I'm just . . . I'm grand.

Medbh   I'm sorry for getting into a snot with you.

Catherine   It's OK. Forget it.

Medbh *kisses her.* **Tom** *stands and goes to the bookshelf.*
Catherine *pulls away from* **Medbh**'s *embrace and sits down.*

Medbh   Do you've any sisters, Tom?

Tom   Five.

Medbh   Ah well. You know what it's like, then.

Tom   What it's like?

Medbh   With sisters. You know.

Tom   Oh yeah. I do all right. There was some rows all right. With five sisters.

He is now at the bookshelf. He takes out a volume. A photograph falls out of it. He picks it up, looks at it . . .

They'd fight like cats in a sack. Sisters. (*He looks at the photo again. To* **Catherine**.) Is this one of you?

Catherine *comes over, smiling.*

Tom   It doesn't look like you. Is that a birthmark there on her forehead? Shaped like . . . a little crescent, isn't it?

When **Catherine** *sees the photo her expression darkens. She snaps it from his hand.*

Medbh (*to* **Catherine**)   Did you find something?

Catherine   Look. A fucking photo of your one. Jesus Christ, if mum had found that.

Medbh   Give it to me.

Catherine *doesn't hand over the photo, but pockets it.*

Catherine   Christ Almighty. Photos of her lying around the place like she was his bloody wife.

Medbh   All right, all right. Calm down, for God's sake.

Catherine   I'm perfectly calm, thank you. I'm fine.

Silence.

What are all the books doing?

Medbh   She's giving them all into UCD. To the library, you know. We're just sorting through them.

Catherine   Is that what he wanted?

Medbh   I don't know. That's what she's doing anyway. She says he was happier in there than he was here.

Catherine   Little does she bloody know. I wouldn't mind looking through them some time.

Medbh   Sure *you* don't read much, do you?

Catherine   Of course I read. Jesus.

Medbh   Oh right. Go ahead if you like. I'm sure she wouldn't mind.

Catherine   Maybe tomorrow.

Medbh   Sure. Why not?

Catherine   So. Any word from the college? About who's coming tomorrow?

Medbh   How do you mean?

Catherine   I mean, did you hear anything? Did anyone say anything to you?

Medbh   About what?

Catherine   About dad. Is your one coming?

Medbh   I don't know what you mean.

Catherine   Look, Medbh, I spoke to Maloney. I rang him up from New York yesterday, and he says there's a rumour going around the college that she's going to turn up tomorrow. Here.

Medbh   Sure, he's only a fucking eejit, Catherine, I didn't hear anything about that. All right?

Catherine   I hope there's no unwelcome guests anyway. I'm going to tell people not to come back to the house afterwards.

Medbh   What? You can't do that, Catherine.

Catherine   I've phoned half of them about it already.

Medbh   What?

Catherine   I'm not having her humiliated, Medbh. If that little bitch is coming along here to cause trouble.

Medbh   What trouble? Don't be so bloody dramatic for God's sake. Look, seriously, I didn't hear anything about it.

Catherine   You didn't talk to Maloney. He said the whole college is talking about it. She's coming tomorrow, I'm telling you. Can you imagine? Playing the spurned fucking mistress in front of mum.

Medbh (*nodding towards* **Tom**)   Look, Catherine. Do we have to talk about this now?

Catherine   It's all right. Tom knows all about it.

Medbh *sighs.*

Medbh   Well, look, let's just leave it for now, all right? She's uptight enough wondering whether Johnny's going to show up.

Catherine   I can't believe he'd even talk about not coming.

Medbh   Well, I rang him and ate the face off him. He said he'd think about it.

Catherine *pours herself a gin and tonic, a whiskey for* **Tom.**

Catherine   They were saying the flights from London were delayed. Out at the airport. We were lucky to get in at all. You should've seen the mist. I've never seen anything like it.

Enter **Moya**, *with a tray of food.*

Moya   Here we are now. Tom, sit up to the table there and you'll have a bite to eat.

Tom   I won't thanks, Mrs Doyle.

Moya   Indeed you will. Sit up there and don't start any trouble. Or will you have it on your lap just?

Tom   Well, all right. Thanks.

Moya *puts the tray on* **Tom***'s lap.*

Moya   I like a man who eats, I must say. My fellow always ate enough for an army. Enda would eat two dinners if he was let and a sweet afterwards, but he never put on too much. No. He was lucky that way.

Tom *begins eating.*

Moya   So where are you from, Tom?

Tom   From Galway, Mrs Doyle.

Moya   Oh call me Moya for God's sake. You make me feel
old with your Mrs Doyle. What part of Galway?

Tom   From Salthill there, Moya.

Moya   Are you really? My people were from Galway I
believe. Before they came up to Dublin and became
Jackeens. They were from near Barna.

Tom   I know Barna well. I'd an aunt married a fellow out
there. Well, from just outside. It's a lovely spot.

Moya   Oh Galway's lovely. We used to go nearly every
year, when these efforts here were small. And then they went
to Irish college there, in Inverin, when they were bigger.
Enda always loved Galway. For a Dublin gurrier, I mean,
although he'd Wexford blood in him too. He used to say he
was a Wexford viking.

Tom   I don't know Wexford. But Galway's all right.

Moya   So you're a Connaught man, that's a turn up. You're
a big secret now to us all. Catherine keeps everything quiet.

Tom   She does yeah. Sometimes.

Medbh   Always did.

Moya   And are you long over in New York?

Tom   Well, I went in '85. I'd a brother over there. In
Queens.

Moya   And do you like it over there?

Tom   I like it well enough, I suppose. There's a lot to do
anyway.

Moya   Oh there is, I believe. I've never been. Enda was
there once for a conference one time. The influence of Yeats
on American culture it was called.

Medbh   Must've been a short fucking conference.

Moya   Medbh, would you stop?

Tom   You'd never be bored in New York anyway. That's the thing.

Moya   Well, it's terrible though, isn't it? The way the young people have to go away now.

Tom   I suppose so.

Medbh   Some of them don't go far enough away, if you ask me.

Moya   It *is* terrible, Medbh.

Medbh (*in her O'Casey voice*)   Ah God, Juno. Sure the whole world's in a terrible state a chassis.

Moya   Listen to that big lump. I can't get her out of the house, Tom, never mind out of the country. If she goes down to the pub on a Friday she nearly sends me a postcard.

Medbh   Stop, you.

Moya   Well, it's true. She's nearly welded into that couch. I don't think it's normal for a girl of her age. Do you think it's normal, Tom? For a girl of her age I mean?

Tom   I don't know.

Moya   Well, I don't think it's normal. Myself and Enda would be stuck in here like Darby and Joan, watching the *Late Late* or something on a Friday, but many's the night the Queen Bee over there wouldn't stir either.

Tom   I don't go out much myself actually.

Catherine (*laughing*)   Yes you do.

Tom   Not that much. I used to go out a lot more.

Catherine   You're always out when I ring you anyway.

Moya   And what does your brother do for a crust over there, Tom?

Tom   He has a bar, Moya. A little place on Second Avenue. The Easter Rising it's called. He's in it nine or ten years now.

Moya   That's great for him. An Irish bar, is it?

Tom   Well, I suppose so. But it's not . . . it's just a bar, you know.

Catherine   It's a gay bar, Mother. Tom's brother is gay.

Moya   Is that right? How interesting.

Catherine   What's interesting about it?

Moya   Well . . . I'm interested, that's all.

Tom   Well, yes. It's not a gay bar as such. We get the odd gay person in there.

Catherine   Listen to him. They're so gay in there their hair is on bloody fire.

Tom   That isn't true now, Catherine.

Catherine   Jesus, they're gay. What's the big deal?

Moya   I used to know quite a few of them. The gay people, you know? I used to act a bit, Tom, when I was younger, and of course you'd meet a lot of them in the theatre. And I always got on well with them. I always found them very funny.

Tom   Really?

Moya   Oh yes. Very humorous.

Tom   I suppose they are.

Moya   Well, they were such gentlemen too, you know. They were good company. I used to pal around with a fellow called Seanie Darcy I think it was. He made costumes in the Gaiety, for the opera especially, when it was on. Such beautiful costumes, all silk, you know, and lace. God, Seanie could make anything with his hands. And he was that way inclined.

Catherine   God Almighty. That way inclined.

Moya   Well he was, dear. And I got an awful fright when he told me first. Just ignorance, you know, because I'd never met one. But I mean we were the best of pals afterwards.

Medbh   What happened to him, Ma?

Moya God I don't know what ever became of Seanie in the end. He had a friend, you know, but he went off to England. The friend. And there was trouble then, because poor Seanie was very upset. There was talk that he took to the drink. Or went to Canada maybe, I can't remember. But Tom, does your brother have a friend?

Tom A friend?

Moya A special friend, you know?

Tom Well, yes, he does.

Moya That's nice for him. Because my poor Seanie, when his friend left him, he was so hurt. And he got a bit bitter then. You know the way they sometimes get a bit like that?

Catherine What are you talking about, Mum?

Moya How do you mean, love?

Catherine 'I'd never met one.' 'You know the way they get bitter.' Good God.

Moya Well, they do. Is that a bad thing to say?

Catherine They do not. For God's sake. No more than anyone else.

Moya Oh well, I didn't say that. But anyway, I remember going to see this play at the Gate once with poor Seanie. It had Hilton Edwards in it and Micheál MacLiammóir, and as you know, they were . . . and anyway, it was called *Home is the Hero*. Oh, it was fabulous now. And in the bar afterwards Seanie says to me, you know, Moya, there was only one little thing wrong with that play, and that was the title. And I said, what, Seanie, *Home is the Hero*? And he said, yes dear, with that pair in it, I thought it should have been called 'Here Is The Homo'.

Tom, Medbh *and* **Catherine** *laugh,* **Catherine** *reluctantly.*

Moya That's a good one isn't it, though?

Tom Did you go to plays with your husband, Moya?

Moya   We went sometimes, dear, but Enda wasn't a great man for the theatre. He'd no patience, God love him. He used to say, the theatre's all very well, but half the time you'd nearly go mad with the feckin' boredom in it.

Tom   Catherine was saying he was a poet.

Moya   Oh well, poet . . . Well, he worked in the library, dear, you know, in UCD. But he wrote poems all right. More when he was younger. More when . . . But he had the occasional one published. He had one in the *Sunday Tribune* last year. It was a bit heavy though. I couldn't really get the meaning of it.

Tom   I'd love to see some of his poems.

Moya   God, I don't even know where they'd be, love. There's a rake of papers to be gone through.

Catherine   I could help you do that.

Moya *caresses* **Catherine***'s face.*

Moya   Of course, love. You can give me all the help you want. I'd like that.

Tom   It must have been interesting, I'd say. Being married to someone who wrote poetry, I mean?

Moya   No. Not really, dear. Enda was always very . . . he kept to himself about it, do you know? He always said he'd write one for me. A love poem, if you don't mind. Oh, the things he was going to say in it, you know yourself. But he never did. Imagine that. All those years together and he never got around to it.

Tom   That's a shame.

Moya   Yes. But who needs poems though, when I have these two ladies? And my son too? Aren't they more a part of him really? When you think. Because I remember a poem Enda showed me once, by Jonson. Ben Jonson, you know. And he says in it that his little son is his greatest work. And

I thought that was lovely, I must say. As a mother, I mean.
I thought that put it very well, the deeper feelings a person
would have, I suppose. And then I thought, my three were
like little poems too.

Medbh Johnny's some poem all right. A terrible fucking
beauty is born.

Moya Listen to that one, Tom. She hasn't a good word for
anyone tonight.

Catherine So what's happening tomorrow, with daddy?

Moya How do you mean?

Catherine Well, is everything taken care of?

Moya Taken care of?

Catherine God, Mum. I mean, is there a grave sorted out
and everything?

Medbh Jesus Christ.

Catherine What? I'm just asking if there's a grave, for
God's sake.

Moya Well, there's something I have to tell you, Catherine.
Your daddy said he wanted to be cremated, love.

Catherine Did he really?

Moya Yes, he did. He said he didn't want to be put into
the ground. He was laughing about it when he said it, but I
knew he meant it. He told me ideally he'd rather we just
lurried him down to Connemara and threw him in an old
potato sack and left him up the side of a mountain for the
eagles to eat. He said to me, Moya, if I'm going into the food
chain, I want to go in that bit higher up than everyone else.

Medbh But then he said he'd settle for cremation.

Moya And he asked me to say, about the ashes, that he
wanted them divided up between the three of you. Between

you and Medbh, and Johnny of course. And Johnny. I know that sounds a bit funny, but that's what he said.

Catherine   Ah Mum, you're not serious?

Moya   Why not?

Medbh   That *is* what he said. He said it to me too.

Catherine   Oh well, I suppose if that's what he wanted.

Catherine *goes to the suitcase full of books and begins rummaging through it.*

Moya   It's a big thing now, Tom, the cremation. It used to be they wouldn't do it in Ireland.

Tom   Why was that?

Moya   God, I don't know. But they wouldn't. Was it against the church or something? I think it might have been. Of course the things that were against the church in those days, you'd need to be up early in the morning to do anything *not* against the church.

Catherine *finds the videos in the suitcase.*

Catherine   What's on these?

Moya   Oh, I don't know, love. I found a load of them in his study the other night. On the top of the wardrobe. There was this big suitcase, you see, and lots of video tapes in it. And then those today. And I've been wondering what to do with them.

Catherine   Have you played them?

Moya   Well, I didn't like to.

Catherine   Why not?

Moya   God, I don't know, really. I thought they might be private.

Catherine   Sure, don't be silly, Mum. Maybe he wanted us to look at them.

Moya   Of course he didn't. Weren't they hidden away?

Catherine   Mum, for God's sake. Maybe he left something behind. Maybe he wanted us to find them. After he was gone.

Medbh   Christ Almighty. You really have been watching too much television.

Catherine   Well, people do that, you know.

Medbh   In your dreams they do.

Moya   I wasn't sure anyway. And I don't really want . . .

Medbh   I'm sure they're just to do with the library, Ma.

Catherine *goes to the video machine, inserts a tape and begins to play it. Her father* **Enda**'s *face appears, speaking intensely.*

Enda   . . . And when I looked at him, I thought, Doctor Malone, you're no friend of mine, and you can keep your bloody advice. And back into the library then. And the conversation was all tripping along quite nicely when Mrs D comes tumbling in pulling out tufts of her blue rinse. Murder over theology . . .

Catherine (*laughing*)   Look! Look, Mum! It's gas, isn't it? Tom, look, there's daddy.

Tom   Yeah. I can see the resemblance all right.

Enda   . . . You see it every year of course, I did warn them this would happen. What happens is, when exams start coming around the damn theology students start borrowing everything in sight and cutting chapters out of them . . .

Catherine *presses stop and takes out the tape.*

Catherine   Do you think they're all of him?

She puts another one in and presses play.

Enda   . . . Big night anyway, went to the faculty end of term brouhaha. The chaplain was there. Father Joe, he insists on being called. One of those trendy ones, liberation theology and so on, bomber jackets, very Nicaragua, intense look, sandals with no socks, moped. I mean it's all very well . . .

Catherine   Is it some kind of diary or what? Have you looked through them properly, Mum?

Medbh *picks up the remote control and presses stop.*

Medbh   I don't want to look at them now.

Catherine   Medbh, I was looking at that . . .

Medbh *nods towards her mother.*

Medbh   Catherine, maybe we'll look at them some other time. Is that OK?

Catherine   Well, yeah. But there's loads of them. Do you think they're all of him? I mean, they'd be worth looking through.

Medbh   Some other time, all right?

Catherine   Jesus, all right, all right. I just thought it was odd, that's all . . . So listen, Mum, when's Johnny coming over?

Moya   God, that *is* gas though, isn't it? Why do you think your father did that? I never knew he did that.

Medbh   Do you not remember, Ma? When he said they got the video camera in the library?

Moya   No. When was that?

Medbh   It was just last year, woman, don't you remember? And he said he'd been messing with it, trying to get it to work and he nearly broke it?

Moya   I don't remember that at all.

Medbh   Good God, Ma. You're little Miss Parallel Universe, aren't you?

Moya   I don't remember that now, I must say.

Catherine   Mum! Johnny. When's he coming over?

Moya   What? Oh, I don't know if he is, love. He's very busy in work. He said he'd try his very best.

Catherine   Busy in work? My God, he's entered the workforce.

Moya   Yes, he's got something working for some outfit or another, some computer place I think it is. But I can't get over that now, your father putting himself on those tape things.

Catherine   Busy in work. I've heard everything now.

Moya   Well, he is very busy now. And you know what he's like. My fellow keeps to himself, Tom. He's a bit like yourself that way, I'd say. Isn't he, Medbh?

Catherine   He is not. Selfish little bastard. He doesn't keep to himself enough for me.

Moya   Don't say that about your brother, love.

Catherine   He is, Mum, and you know it.

Moya *looks at her watch.*

Moya   Well, I don't know if he's coming now. I suppose the last of the flights'd be in now. Or maybe we could ring the airport?

Medbh   They'd be in, Ma. There's no point.

Catherine   So. Which room do you want to put us in?

Moya   Who, love?

Catherine   Myself and Tom, of course.

Moya   Yourself and Tom?

Catherine   Well, unless Gabriel Byrne shows up, myself and Tom, yes.

Moya (*forced laughter*)   God, it's great now, isn't it, for you youngsters. Which room do you want us in? Your poor father not even buried and his house already turning into the Folies Bergères.

Catherine Mum, look, we're sleeping together, all right, and we're over the age of consent, so I mean . . .

Tom (*embarrassed*) Catherine, for God's sake.

Moya Oh, you needn't lecture me about it, now. You're big and bold enough to do what you want, so I'm not arguing. I'm only saying.

Catherine Well, let's not have a big debate over it.

Moya God Almighty, sure, I'm only jealous. Come on then and help me make up the bed.

Moya *and* **Catherine** *leave.* **Tom** *and* **Medbh** *are apprehensive of each other.*

Medbh You're red in the face, Tom.

Tom Am I? God.

Medbh Don't worry. Ma loves the slagging. She wouldn't mean any harm.

Tom Oh no, I know that.

Silence.

So. You're Medbh anyway.

Medbh I am, yeah.

Tom You're Medbh. I've heard a lot about you.

Medbh And the rest of the family too, it seems. Well, I've heard nothing at all about you, Tom.

Tom Catherine talks about you a lot, so she does.

Medbh Really? What does she say?

Tom Just, you know. She talks about you. She's gas when she gets talking. You wouldn't get a word in.

Medbh *and* **Tom** *speak simultaneously.*

Medbh ⎫ What does she say though?
Tom   ⎭ It's hard to think of what . . .

Medbh (*laughs*)   Sorry.

Tom   No. Go on.

Medbh   You were telling me what she says.

Tom   What she says?

Medbh   About me.

Tom   Oh yes. About you. Well, she says you're a very strong person. Very steady.

Medbh (*laughs*)   God, does she?

Tom   And she says you're very brainy. And you were very good at your studies. She says you're ate with brains. Like your da.

Medbh *laughs.*

Tom   What?

Medbh   It's just your expression. What was it?

Tom   Ate with brains? My mother used to say that to us. Don't pretend to be a big thick, she'd say, you're ate with brains.

Medbh   It's nice.

Tom   I suppose it's a bit stupid.

Medbh   No, it's lovely. So how long have you known her now?

Tom   My mother?

Medbh (*laughs*)   No. Catherine. How long are you an item now?

Tom   I suppose it's, what is it now? A year nearly. The best part of a year.

Medbh   God Almighty, you must be some sort of saint, Tom.

Tom   I don't know about that.

Medbh   You'll get a lot of time off your spell in purgatory for putting up with that one.

Tom   I don't know. I'm fairly mad about her anyway. She made a great difference to me, you know. When I met her.

Medbh   She's all right, I suppose.

Tom   She's a very strong person herself. Very considerate. She lets on to be an awful wagon sometimes, but she's a heart the size of a lorry. And she's a great dancer too.

Medbh   Really? I never knew that.

Tom   Oh God, yeah. Catherine? I met her in this place in New York called Rhinestone Cowboys, it's a line dancing place, you know. I used to go with a crowd, on a Monday, girls and fellas together, you know, just for the crack. And that's where I met her.

Medbh   I wouldn't've had Lady Jane down as a line dancer.

Tom   Oh no, she hates it. She likes the rap music, you know, and rave music. She was only working there.

Medbh   She was working there?

Tom   She was waitressing, yeah.

Medbh   Was she? I thought she was working for some lawyer.

Tom   Was she?

Medbh   That's what she said. She was working for some lawyer. The office was in the Empire State Building.

Tom   Well, she was working in Rhinestone Cowboys when I met her. And we just clicked I suppose.

Medbh   Well, she looks well on it anyway.

Tom It's gas about them videos, isn't it? Your mother seemed a bit uneasy about playing them.

Medbh Yeah. Well. I suppose it's a bit strange for her.

Tom Sure, of course it would be. Were you close to your dad?

Medbh We had our ups and downs, you know, in the family. (*She laughs.*) I guess you do know, since blabberbeak upstairs told you.

Tom Every family has them though. And I suppose you don't want to be thinking about them at a time like this.

Medbh No. Exactly.

Silence.

Tom It's a terrible thing for you all anyway.

Medbh Yeah. Listen, Tom, you're very good to come over.

Tom Well, I wouldn't let herself come over on her own. Because I remember my own father dying. He died when I was only eight, you know. And my uncle said to me, the day we buried him, Tom, this is the worst day of your life. And it's important that somebody says that to you. This is the worst day of your life, son, and you'll never really forget today.

Catherine *comes back in.*

Catherine Well. You two look like you're getting along well.

Tom We are. Sure, why wouldn't we be?

Catherine Is she flirting with you, Tom? Medbh's an awful flirt, everyone says it.

Medbh Shut up you, you'd get up on a stiff breeze.

Catherine Do you want another drink, Tom?

Tom All right.

She pours him another whiskey, makes another gin for herself.

Medbh   So how's the Empire State Building anyway?

Catherine   How do you mean?

Medbh   How's your office, in the Empire State Building?

Tom   That's not where your office is, is it?

Catherine   No it isn't. It's on 46th and Eighth. Sure, you know that.

Medbh   You wrote to ma that you were working in the Empire State Building.

Catherine (*laughs*)   No, I didn't.

Medbh   You did, Catherine. I mean I don't care or anything. But you did say that. You said you were working in a lawyer's office in the Empire State Building and that you could see all the way down to the Statue of Liberty from your window.

Catherine   You're dreaming, Medbh. I never said that.

Medbh   Catherine, for fuck's sake, you know you did.

Catherine   I did not.

Enter **Moya**.

Moya   Well, I don't know about anyone else, but I'm bushed now.

Catherine   Would you not go on up to bed, Mum?

Moya *looks at her watch.*

Moya   Ah, I think I'll wait up a little more. There might be a film on or something. They sometimes have an old film, Tom, on ITV late at night. I love the old black and white films.

Medbh   Ma, it's well after midnight.

Moya   Go on. Leave me here. I'll be fine.

Catherine   You shouldn't be by yourself.

Moya   Go on, for God's sake. I'm not a baby.

Medbh   I'll stay up for a while anyway. I'm not tired.

Catherine (*to* **Tom**)   Will we head up, so?

Tom   OK.

Tom *gulps down his drink.* **Catherine** *kisses her mother.*

Catherine   Good night, Mum. Try to get some sleep.

Moya   Good night, pet. Oh I'll sleep all right, never fear. I don't have a fine big hunk like Tom to keep me awake.

Catherine   Mum!

Tom   Good night, Moya.

Moya   Good night now, love. It's lovely to have you here with us.

Tom *and* **Catherine** *leave.*

Moya   Well, what do you reckon?

Medbh   He seems all right.

Moya   Do you think? There's no sign of a ring anyway.

Medbh   I'm sure you had a good look.

Moya   Mmmm. We're not exactly weighed down with the brains, are we?

Medbh   Don't be such a wagon, will you?

Moya   Sure, once they're happy I suppose.

Medbh   Jesus, Ma, if I ever bring a fella back here and you say that I'll brain you with a shovel.

Moya   What?

Medbh   So long as they're happy. Why don't you just say he's thick as shite in a bucket and be done with it?

Moya   I'm not saying that. Now. Put another one of those videos on.

Medbh   Are you sure?

Moya   Yes. I'd like to see him now. But do you think there's anything to what Catherine was saying though? Do you think there's something important on them?

Medbh   Not at all, Ma. I think he was just messing.

Moya   It's curious, though, isn't it? Put one on anyway.

Medbh *inserts a tape and turns on the video. She opens a can of beer for herself and pours a whiskey for her mother.*

Enda *can be seen again, his face close to the screen as he switches on the camera. He walks away from it and sits down in a chair behind a desk. He runs his fingers through his hair.*

Medbh   Where's that? Is that his office, Ma?

Moya   God, I don't know. I was never in it in my life.

Enda   Hello? Hello there? Testing one, two, three.

Moya   Look at the get-up of him. It's gas, isn't it?

Suddenly **Enda** *begins clicking his fingers like a singer from the Swing era. He sways his shoulders from side to side and begins imitating the sound of an orchestra.*

Moya   God Almighty. What's he doing, Medbh?

Medbh   Jesus. Is he going mad?

Enda *starts singing in exaggerated Las Vegas-style: 'Heartbreak Hotel'.*

Medbh *and* **Moya** *laugh all the way through the song.* **Enda** *suddenly loses his place in it. He scratches his head.*

Enda   What's the blasted words to that anyway?

He approaches the camera and turns it off. Screen goes to white noise. Room goes to darkness.

White noise dissolves into the sound of the sea, waves breaking on rocks.

Lights up as **Young Moya** *runs on. She hides behind a pillar.*

Young Enda (*offstage*)   Moya, Moya. Where are you? Come and look at the sea.

Enter **Young Enda**. *He's breathless.*

Young Enda   Where've you gone, Moya?

Young Moya *jumps out.*

Young Moya   Here! Are you blind as well as daft, Enda Doyle?

They laugh and hug.

Young Enda   God Almighty, you're always running away from me. I think you don't love me at all.

Young Moya   I never said I did, did I?

Young Enda   You don't. You've clicked with someone else, my girl.

Young Moya   Oh, you'd love to be rid of me so easily.

Young Enda   Stop that talk. I'll always be here. You know that.

Young Moya   You're only saying it to get on my soft side.

Young Enda   Do you know what day it is today? It's the fifteenth of June, 1964. Do you know what that means? We're together three whole months today. And you forgot.

Young Moya   Of course I knew that, you lump.

Young Enda   And I'm after getting you a present too. Here. Close your eyes first.

Young Moya *closes her eyes and holds out her hands. He takes her hands and kisses her on the lips.*

Young Moya   Stop that messing, you scut, or you'll be sorry.

Young Enda   No, here. Close your eyes again.

He gives her a brown paper bag which contains an old book.

Young Moya   God. What is it?

Young Enda   Can you not read, love? It's *The Love Songs of Connaught*, by Douglas Hyde, the first President of Ireland. It's the most beautiful magical book, Moya. And that copy's nearly a hundred years old.

Young Moya   Is it really? Well, aren't you the awful fool wasting your money on something like that.

Young Enda   Mr Cohen in the shop said I could have it on the never never. It's so lovely and old. He got it from an old lady who came in, and she got it from her grandmother! And I'd wish you all the happiness and all the dreams and all the love . . . all the hopes that anyone ever felt who held that book in their hands, Moya. And more.

Young Moya   I'll clatter you in a minute. The way you talk.

Young Enda   It's so beautiful though. Look at this one here.

He leafs through the book, looking for a poem.

My grief on the sea
How the waves of it roll
As it comes between me and the love of my soul.

Isn't that just gorgeous, Moya? That's how I feel about you. When I'm away from you.

Young Moya   God Almighty, the rubbish you go on with. And you needn't think you'll plamas me so easily. I'm not one of your English ones whose head you'll turn playing the poor Irish gom.

They hug again.

Young Enda   God help me. I'm completely at your mercy.

Young Moya   Oh listen. The dying swan.

Young Enda   And I'll always be here to help you.

Young Moya   I'm sure you will. Till the right girl comes along. If you haven't got her stashed away somewhere already.

Young Enda   Are you astray in the head or what? I'll always love you, Moya Rogan, I cross my heart and hope to die.

Lights up suddenly on the living-room. **Medbh** *is asleep on the couch. The video is playing again, with the sound turned down so that* **Enda**'s *voice is a barely audible mumble.* **Moya** *is watching it. She stands, goes to the window, looks out. She glances at her watch, peers through the window again. Then she sighs and closes the curtains. She goes to* **Medbh** *and shakes her gently a few times.* **Medbh** *remains asleep.* **Moya** *laughs softly. She looks around for something to cover her with. She takes her husband's coat down from its hanger on the door and puts it over her daughter.*

Moya *goes to the video machine and kneels down. She cannot bring herself to turn it off. She touches the screen for a moment, but leaves the tape playing. She stands again. She turns off the lights and leaves the room. The room is dark now, except for* **Enda**'s *face on the video, which fades slowly to complete darkness. Sound of funeral bells.*

Act Two

Sound of funeral bells continues. Lights up on the living-room, with daylight through the window. The room is piled high with sandwiches and drink, as before. The only difference is that the piles of books have been removed to the corners, the tea chests and suitcase have been placed behind the sofa, and perhaps a dozen chairs have been arranged around the room. A video tape of **Enda** *speaking is playing, with no sound.*

Enter **Moya, Medbh, Tom** *and* **Catherine** *all dressed in black.* **Catherine** *is holding her mother's hand.* **Moya** *is carrying an urn.* **Moya** *looks at the video screen.*

Moya (*to* **Medbh**)   Did you leave that on, love? When we went out?

Medbh   No. I didn't go near it.

Catherine   Neither did I.

Moya   Sure, somebody must have.

Tom   I could've sworn it was off when we left for the church. I thought I checked it.

Moya   Well, it didn't switch itself on, did it?

They look at each other and shrug. **Medbh** *switches the machine off.* **Moya** *goes into the kitchen. The others take off their coats and sit down.* **Medbh** *hangs the coats up. (Her father's coat is back hanging on the door.) She prepares a round of drinks and hands them around. Then she sits down too. Silence for some moments.* **Catherine** *lights a cigarette.*

Catherine   That's strange though, isn't it?

Tom   What, pet?

Catherine   The video being on.

Tom   I must be wrong. I mustn't have checked it.

Catherine   Sure, I saw you. You turned off the plug.

Tom   That's what I thought. But I mustn't have.

Catherine You did, Tom. You know, I've read about things like this.

Tom Like what?

Catherine Paranormal things.

Tom Would you stop messing for God's sake?

Catherine I read an article about it. They say when a person dies, and if they've left something unfinished . . . if their aura doesn't want to return to the void it can stay behind. Here.

Tom Would you cut it out, Catherine? Their aura.

Catherine Well, that's what I read. If there's something the person should've done, and they didn't do it, some of their energy stays behind. In the place where they lived, or the place they worked, and . . .

Tom Catherine, stop it now.

Catherine Well, how would you explain it?

Tom I just turned off the wrong plug.

Catherine (*laughing*) You didn't, Tom. You know you didn't.

He ignores her. Silence.

Catherine So. Did you see her there in the church?

Medbh Leave it, will you.

Catherine The way she went on. Moaning and crying like that. Jesus.

Medbh Catherine, please.

Catherine She better not turn up here, I'll tell you that much.

Medbh *ignores her and concentrates on her drink.*

Medbh Well, it was a lovely mass.

Catherine God Almighty, I thought it was awful.

Tom It was grand, I thought.

Catherine   The priest was a bit cringe-making wasn't he?

Tom   I thought he was sound as a hound.

Catherine   God is like a librarian? On the last day he'll gather up all the books and put them on the one heavenly shelf? I mean, Jesus Christ, is that out of a Daniel O'Donnell song?

Medbh   It's from John Donne actually. One of his sermons. It was one of dad's favourites. Did you not know that?

Catherine   Was it? Well, I thought it was morbid. And that folk group, strumming away like that. He's got the whole world in his hands. God, it was embarrassing. I mean half of them were wearing trainers. And the acne on the altar boy. He looked like he'd shaved himself with a fucking cheese grater. And when we went to the crematorium, Jesus.

Medbh   What?

Catherine   I mean the tape playing 'Bridge Over Troubled Waters' when they put the coffin in.

Medbh   Well, what did you want? 'Come On Baby, Light My Fire'?

Catherine   I thought your one would have to be fucking hospitalised at that stage, the big act she put on.

Medbh   Catherine . . .

Moya *suddenly comes back in, carrying three lunch boxes and a large spoon.*

Moya   Well, I've a job to do now, before everyone arrives.

Catherine   What?

Moya   I've a promise to keep. I have to divide up the ashes.

Catherine   God, Mum. Do you have to do it now?

Moya   Why not?

Catherine   Couldn't we do it later?

Moya   We'll do it now, and that'll be an end to it.

She places the urn on a table and unscrews the lid. She reaches into the urn with the spoon, takes out a handful and begins to fill up the lunch boxes.

Come on now. Gather round.

Catherine Jesus, Mum, you can't do that.

Moya What?

Catherine You can't put daddy into a bloody lunch box.

Moya Well, I've nothing else, dear.

They watch with a mixture of horror and fascination while **Moya** *performs the operation.*

Medbh Which one's mine?

Moya (*pointing*) That one.

Medbh How come you're giving her more than me? Gimme a bit more.

Moya Would you have a bit of respect, for God's sake.

Medbh (*fighting back laughter*) Sorry, Ma.

Moya *continues the delicate operation.*

Medbh Can I lick the spoon?

Moya Medbh Doyle, I'll skelp you in a minute.

Catherine Well, I don't care. I'm not bringing daddy back to New York in a lunch box. Tom, hand me over my bag, will you?

Tom *retrieves the handbag.* **Medbh** *puts the other two lunch boxes on a shelf out of the way.*

Moya (*nodding at handbag*) You're not putting him in that?

Medbh (*in* Lady Bracknell *mode*) A handbag?

Moya (*to* **Medbh**) Would you stop it?

Catherine Of course I'm not.

She takes an envelope out of her bag. She pours the ashes from the lunch box into the envelope. She peers into it.

It's hard to believe that's all that's left of him.

Moya   Well, that isn't all that's left, love. I mean, we remember him, don't we? That's the important thing.

Catherine   Well, I know that.

Moya   And aren't you here? Big lump?

Catherine   I suppose so.

Moya *kisses her.* **Catherine** *puts the envelope back into her bag.*

Moya   As long as I have you, he'll never be gone. Isn't that right, Tom?

Tom   That's right, Moya.

Behind them, from the interior of the house, **Johnny** *enters, naked except for a bathtowel and underpants. He is carrying the rest of his clothes over his arm.*

Johnny   Well well.

They whip round.

Moya (*startled*)   Jesus! Johnny! Oh Johnny, son.

Johnny   What a pretty picture. The Catholic family united in grief. How are you, Maw?

Moya   Oh Johnny. It's so lovely to see you. You gave me an awful start.

Johnny   I let myself in. Hope you don't mind. I was just taking a shower.

They embrace. **Moya** *buries her face in his shoulder.*

Moya   Johnny, it's just lovely to see you, son. You put the heart crossways in me.

Johnny   And grand to see you too, little grey-haired Mother.

Moya   Oh Johnny, son.

Johnny   And look, sweet Jesus, the two ugly sisters as well.
My God, everyone's here. And even The Da's here, on the
silver screen anyway.

Moya   Was that you switched it on?

Johnny   Who else? Good old Enda, eh? Tripping the light
fantastic. I've been watching them all morning and he didn't
crack one fucking joke.

Medbh   Catherine thought they were a message from
daddy.

Johnny   Well, she would. Wouldn't you, pet?

Catherine   I didn't say that.

Moya   But could you not have got over earlier, love? You're
after missing everything. What kept you?

Johnny *begins to dress himself.*

Johnny   I got tied up, Ma. Jenny tied me up.

Moya   You're a terrible brat. Would you cover yourself up,
for God's sake, I was long enough looking at you. I knew
you'd be here though. I said a little prayer last night and I
knew you'd be here.

Johnny   Very good.

Moya   Didn't I say that to you, Medbh? That he'd be here.

Medbh   Yeah, you did.

Johnny   And you were right. Now. Any chance of a drink
there, Mother?

Moya   Of course, love. What would you like?

Johnny (*nodding at* **Tom**)   Who's this? I'll have a whiskey.

Moya   Are you sure now? You wouldn't rather a glass of
milk?

Johnny   I'm sure, Mother dear.

Moya *pours him a large glass of whiskey and hands it over.*

Catherine   Johnny, this is Tom. Tom, this is my brother, Johnny.

They shake hands.

Johnny   Tom, Tom, the piper's son. I'm thrilled to meet you, Tom. Tell us, do you pluck your eyebrows?

Tom   Sorry?

Johnny   Tweezers, you know. Do you pluck your eyebrows?

Tom   No I don't.

Moya   Don't be ridiculous, love. Of course he doesn't.

Johnny   Really? Well they're very beautiful, Tom, if I may say so. You'd want to see the eyebrows on some of the creatures that sister of mine has brought strolling in here through the years. Jesus Christ, one of them just had one big eyebrow across his forehead. He was like something out of the circus. He was like a big fucking muppet in a Dunnes Stores' suit.

Tom   Is that right?

Catherine   Don't mind him, Tom.

Moya   No, don't, Tom. You leave Tom alone, you brat. Oh now, look, there's no ice. Wait till I get some.

Medbh   I'll get it, Ma.

Moya   No no. I'll get it.

Moya *leaves.* **Johnny** *goes to the bookshelf with his glass.*

Johnny   So. How was it?

Medbh   You could have been there.

Johnny   I got held up.

Medbh   What are you talking about?

Johnny   I got held up in London.

Medbh   My arse. You would have been here if you wanted to be.

Johnny   Well, I don't like funerals. I'm not the type.

Catherine   It would have meant a lot to her.

Johnny *sits down on the sofa with a book in his hands.*

Johnny   So, Tom. I suppose you've fucked my sister?

Medbh   Jesus, Johnny.

Tom   Sorry?

Johnny   You heard me, Tommo. You and sis there, have you been looking at the mantlepiece or stoking the fire? I actually prefer looking at the mantlepiece myself. I mean most fireplaces look the same after a while, don't you think, Tom?

Tom   I don't know. I don't know what you mean.

Johnny   Oh, we don't know. We're not allowed to have an opinion, no? By the creature from the fucking black lagoon over there?

Catherine   Don't mind him, Tom. Johnny specialises in trying to be outrageous. It's because he has no friends.

Johnny   That's right. No friends.

Catherine   No friends. No prospects. No nothing.

Johnny   Not like you, dear.

Catherine   That's right. Not like me.

Johnny   That's right, Tom. Not like Catherine, the most popular girl in the class.

Catherine   Fuck off.

Medbh   Don't start, the pair of you.

Johnny   And such a command of the English language. What a tongue.

Medbh   Johnny, please.

Johnny   A lot of people have been on the receiving end of that tongue of course. But we don't talk about that.

Medbh   Johnny!

Johnny   Well, anyway, here's to innocence.

He drains his glass and pours another. Silence in the room while he thumbs through a book.

Johnny (*reading*)   'It is now sixteen or seventeen years since I saw the Queen of France, then the Dauphiness, at Versailles, and surely never lighted on this orb . . .' Orb? Jesus. Orb?

He throws the book down.

Orb my bollix.

Silence.

So. Will we check out of a bit more of the old video collection? The message from beyond the grave?

Catherine   Fuck off.

Johnny *laughs.*

Tom   So, Johnny. Is it London?

Johnny   Is what London?

Tom   Is that where you are? I mean, where you're living?

Johnny   It is where I am, yes. You could say that, though I don't know if you'd call it living. But anyway, no, nice try, Thomas, but back to the point. I suppose you've given her the old lash by now, have you?

Tom   I don't really think you should talk about your sister like that.

Johnny   Oh, oh. Naughty boy. Nice little Tom doesn't think I should talk about my sister like that.

Catherine   You're a fucking pitiful bollocks you know. You always were and you always will be.

Medbh   Catherine, please.

Johnny I'm only joking, Jesus. Smile and give your face a fucking holiday.

Catherine You're not funny.

Johnny Tom, I say, old man, I'm most awfully sorry. Truly. Je suis desolée.

Tom No, you're all right.

Johnny (*to* **Catherine**) See? I'm sorry, and all's forgiven.

Catherine *says nothing.*

Johnny And Sister Medbh the Rave. How's that long streak of misery of yours? Jerry from Kerry? With his brother Terry?

Medbh We broke up.

Johnny Good Christ! Tom and Jerry. That's just occurred to me. You're getting up to mischief with a Tom, apparently, and you, for your part, are fucking a Jerry.

Medbh We broke up.

Johnny Tom and shagging Jerry. My God, if I could only find Minnie Mouse, we'd be laughing.

Medbh More like the hundred and one dalmatians in your case.

Johnny Very good, my dear. Yes, there've been a few canines, I have to admit, a few crufts champions over the years. Your Jerry, however, is such a prime fucking specimen of Chippendale manhood, isn't he?

Medbh We split up, I told you.

Johnny Oh yes. You split up. The path of true love, of course, it never did run smooth, did it? The path of love is bent as a Monahan road.

Medbh It is indeed.

Johnny And twice as full of potholes.

Medbh I'm sure this is all very boring for poor Tom.

Tom No, no. I'm fine.

Johnny   No, no. Poor Tom should know. We're not very good at relationships, Tom, in our little clan. It's all to do with our difficult childhoods, you see. My psychiatrist was only telling me the other day. There I am, whinging on his couch, you know, and he says, Johnny, those voices you keep hearing, Johnny, they don't mention anything about my fee, do they? And then he says, you have difficulty bonding. Bonding. And I don't like that word. It makes me think of superglue. It makes me think of handcuffs and chains and big women with leather tits, Tom, what does it make you think of?

Tom   I don't really know.

Johnny   Yes. What a surprise. Tom doesn't really know. Well, big German woman with nipples like organ stops is what it makes me think of, and I say all this to Doctor Murphy, the Sigmund Freud of Palmers Green and he says it's all Mater and Pater's fault. Old Catherine there would have loved him. She thinks everything is Mater and Pater's fault too, don't you dear?

Catherine   Shut up, Johnny. For Christ's sake.

Johnny   No no, let's remember the dead. Here's to the faithful departed. From me and my inner child.

Johnny *takes another large slug from his glass, then refills it again.*

Medbh   Not today, Johnny. Please.

Johnny   Yes, you're right. We don't want to put Tom off now, do we? He looks like a promising one, the latest in a very long line of course, but a good one. And I mean, all right, our dear sister has been through a few hands but who can blame her? Because you have to kiss a lot of frogs before you find your handsome prince. Isn't that right, dear? Or am I embarrassing you?

Catherine   You're embarrassing yourself.

Johnny   We've kissed some frogs, have we not? We've trawled through the old swamp in our time, searching for Kermit on fifty grand a year.

Moya *comes in with a saucer of ice and an ice bucket. She puts the ice bucket on a table and comes to* **Johnny**.

Moya   Now. (*She pours ice from the saucer into his glass.*) There you are. Would you not have a sandwich, pet? You're looking fierce thin.

Johnny   I'm not looking thin, Mother.

Moya   Indeed you are. God, look at you. You'd see more meat on a butcher's bike on a Friday afternoon. That Jenny isn't feeding you properly. Is she coming over so I can tear a strip off her?

Johnny   She can't, Ma. She's not well.

Moya (*demeanour changes*)   What's wrong with her?

Johnny   Well, you're not to throw the head, but she had an accident the other day.

Moya   Oh my God, you didn't tell me that.

Johnny   I didn't want to worry you, Ma.

Moya   Johnny, for God's sake. Was it serious?

Johnny   Well, it is serious actually. She was over in Paris on work you see, for a few days, and she's in the office anyway and she hears bells, outside in the street. An ice-cream van. And she fancies an ice cream. Because it's a hot day. So out she goes. And wham. She gets run over. By the fucking ice-cream van. They had to amputate her leg.

Moya   Jesus, you're joking me.

Johnny   No I'm not. They had to amputate her leg. Up to the thigh.

Moya   My God Almighty. The poor dote.

Johnny   Yes. I got this message in the office, and it didn't even say which fucking leg. And I had to ring the hospital in Paris to ask. And I don't speak very good French, you know? I mean, Quelle jambe, Monsieur le Docteur? Le droit ou le gauche? Is that right? I mean, the leaving cert doesn't really prepare you for these situations, does it?

Catherine   I don't know how *you'd* know.

Johnny   What?

Catherine   About the leaving cert. Since you failed yours twice.

Johnny   Oh thanks a lot. Here I am pouring out my heart about my poor crippled girlfriend . . .

Tom   Jesus. That's terrible though.

Moya   Sacred Heart.

Tom   That's really terrible.

Johnny   It is. Oh, it is.

He bows his head as though he is about to cry. He puts his hand to his face. Suddenly he starts hopping up and down on one leg. He collapses with laughter.

Ah Joxer, she gave her leg for Auld Ireland! Look at the fucking mugs on you.

Medbh (*throws a cushion at him*)   You poxy bastard.

Moya   You dirty gurrier. How is she really?

Johnny   She's fine, Mother. Still driving me around the bend, of course, still spreading my balls on toast.

Moya   One leg indeed. I didn't believe you for a minute. And when are you going to marry the poor girl?

Johnny   The poor girl doesn't want to get married, Mother. These London girls never want to get married, God love and preserve them. It's something in the water over there. And neither do I. It's a perfect arrangement.

Moya   Oh well. We'll see about that now. Tom, this fellow of mine doesn't believe in marriage. Did you ever hear the like?

Tom   I didn't, no.

Johnny Oh, I believe in marriage, Tom. I mean if I'm going to get old and sad and fat anyway, I'm bloody well taking somebody with me.

Moya We'll see. You'll want to get married when you have kids.

Johnny Yes. Well, don't hold your breath, Mother.

Moya *looks at her watch.*

Moya God now, I can't understand why nobody's here. I suppose they're still in the pub.

Johnny They'll be here, Mother, don't worry.

Catherine I think it's all nonsense anyway, this coming back to the house afterwards.

Moya Ah, it's not, love. People want to pay their respects.

Catherine I think it's nonsense. I'd be just as happy if they all left us alone.

Johnny Would you really?

Catherine I would actually.

Johnny Really? You don't think they'd like to come around and see what The Da has to tell us all on the old posthumous video, no?

Catherine You're hilarious. You really are.

Johnny Well, I had a wonderful taxi driver from the airport anyway. He had one of those things on his seat. With the beads, you know. And I said, is that any good? And he said, oh yeah, it is, pal. It stops you sweatin'. Because in the summer, the heat does be fuckin' dreadful. And the shirt does be stickin' to the seat. And the sweat, my Jayzus, does be rollin' down yer back. And it gathers there, in the small of yer back, and it trickles down between yer cheeks. And I do have piles, yeh see, terrible piles, and sweat, by its very nature, is salty. That's what he said to me. Sweat, by its very nature, is salty. And it does tear the arse ourra yeh.

Everyone laughs.

Moya   Isn't that lovely talk, Tom?

Catherine   Will you leave Tom alone, for God's sake?

Moya   What?

Catherine   You're asking the poor man to do a running commentary on everything.

Moya   God, I am not. Am I, Tom?

Tom   Not at all, Moya.

Johnny   Well, here we are all together. Anyone know any jokes?

Catherine   I don't think it's a very good time for jokes.

Johnny   Oh really? Well, Jesus is walking down the road one day . . . and he meets this adulteress. And . . .

Medbh   Johnny.

Johnny   What? It's a good Catholic joke too.

Moya   All the same. If you don't mind.

Johnny   And there I was on the plane thinking, thank God I'm going home to dear auld holy Ireland, where I can tell my Catholic joke and people will get it. They don't get it over in England, you see, being a shower of Proddy pagans.

Tom   I wonder would I get it?

Moya   And why wouldn't you, love?

Tom   Because I'm a Protestant.

Johnny   Are you, Tom? But you're from the countryside, aren't you?

Tom   I'm from Galway.

Johnny   And do they have Protestants in the countryside?

Moya   Of course they do, my God.

Johnny   Really? Well, take me back to Tennessee. And do you live in one of those big houses?

Tom   What?

Johnny   You know, those big houses that country Protestants live in? The ones they used to write the novels about. Skulduggery in the Scullery.

Tom   No we don't.

Johnny   Burnt down, I suppose.

Tom   What?

Johnny   Burnt down in the liberation struggle. The struggle for Irlanda Libre?

Tom   No.

Johnny   Fell down of its own accordion.

Medbh   Will you shut the fuck up, you big eejit?

Silence. **Medbh** *makes more drinks and hands them around.* **Moya** *looks at her watch.*

Moya   God, it's nearly four already. I think I'll just go out to the road and see if anyone's coming.

Johnny   Will I go with you, Ma?

Moya   Not at all love, I'm fine. You stay here.

Moya *throws on her coat and goes out. Silence in the room.*

Johnny   So. Are the two ugly sisters going to tell me why nobody's here?

Catherine   I don't know.

Johnny   I see. So. Catherine's the eldest anyway, Tom. She was The Da's pet. She used to look after us, didn't you, Catherine?

Tom   Is that right?

Johnny   Yes, that's right. But she wouldn't remember. She used to look after us when our parents went out. She was always the pet, you see. But she wouldn't remember looking after us.

Catherine   I do remember.

Johnny   She used to slap us around the place when our parents were out, didn't you? It was before she went into therapy and discovered her inner feelings.

Catherine   I did not.

Johnny   Oh she did. Before she learnt how to validate her anger and express her assertiveness. Back then she used to validate her anger by kicking seven shades of shite out of us, Tom. Her little power thing, you know. She used to get off on it. I remember the look in her eyes when she used to do it, you've probably seen it yourself, Tom, from time to time, or at least I hope you have.

Tom   She's a bit fierce sometimes all right.

Johnny   She is, as you say, a bit fierce sometimes, Tom, the way the Reverend Ian Paisley is a bit fierce sometimes. She used to get on top of me with her legs on each side of my chest, you know the way, Tom, and she'd slap the face off me.

Catherine   I never did that.

Johnny   And sometimes she'd wait till her friends were here, and she'd do it then. She'd sit on top of me, with her legs over my chest, you know? And you know what she's like, Tom, when she has her legs over a person's chest.

Catherine *is now upset and fighting back tears.*

Medbh   Leave her alone, why don't you?

Johnny   That's exactly the way I'm going to fucking leave her, don't worry. That's exactly the way she'll end up.

Catherine *begins to cry.*

Johnny   Smoke gets in your eyes, darling. Occupational hazard for a martyr.

Medbh   Stop it. Can't you see she's upset?

Johnny   I wonder, I wonder, said the duke to the dame, why they all threw a wake, but sure nobody came.

Catherine   You don't care about anyone's suffering, do you?

Johnny   You think you've a monopoly on suffering. You think you fucking invented it.

Catherine   It's just perfect for you, isn't it? Scrutinising the fucking world from that armchair. Why don't you just crawl into your bottle and stay there?

Moya *comes back, in time to hear the end of* **Catherine**'s *last outburst.*

Moya   Will you stop it! Will you stop accusing each other.

Silence. **Johnny** *pours himself another large drink. He lights a cigarette.*

Johnny   I'm sorry.

Moya   Good God, what are you like? I don't know what your father would say if he was here.

Johnny   I know what he'd say. He'd say nothing.

Moya   What do you mean?

Johnny   He'd say nothing, the way he always did when there was something on his mind. And then he'd stand up and put on his jacket and he'd say he was going out. The way he always did.

Moya   You're very hard on him.

Johnny   Oh yeah, sure. Very hard. First sign of trouble, Tom. On your marks, Daddy. Get set, Daddy. Go, Daddy. Like Linford Christie out that door. Unless it was Catherine, of course. Anything for Catherine, but me and Medbh? Out that door and head for the hills.

Moya   Please, Johnny, don't talk like that.

Johnny   Oh right, he was a fucking saint, was he?

Moya   There's few enough of us are saints.

Johnny   He sure wasn't one anyway.

Moya   He wouldn't have claimed to be.

Johnny   He wouldn't have claimed anything. He would have waited for the rest of us to find out.

Moya   You know, Johnny, I sometimes wonder whether I was married to the same man you talk about.

Johnny   As well you might.

Moya   You seem full of terrible stories about him. I don't know where you get them.

Johnny   Oh really, Ma. Don't you? Well, let's tell a few stories, will we? Seeing as nobody knows any jokes. I'll start. I used to rob shops, Tom, when I was a kid. My very expensive psychiatrist has explained to me that this was all my parents' fault, because they didn't give me enough attention. But I didn't know that at the time. I thought I used to rob shops because I was a robbing pure little bastard. But there I am anyway, in Eason's, one day, and up the jumper goes this big book of poetry. Yeats's poems. Father's Day is coming up, you see, and I've no readies for a present for The Da, so. Up the ganzee goes Willie B. And I'm on my way out the door, tap on the shoulder. Up to the manager's office quick march. Why did you do it, says he. I'm disturbed, says I. The manager rings up The Da. The Da comes in firing on all cylinders, guns blazing, I mean, open for fuckin' business, Tom. He bet me from one end of Abbey Street to the other. And do you know what he did then?

Tom   What?

Johnny   He took me down to the cop shop himself.

Moya   Stop, Johnny.

Johnny   Down to Store Street. And I'm crying. I mean, I'm seven. And I'm so scared that I'm pissing in my pants, Tom. And I'm begging. Please, Daddy, please, I'll never do it again. And what does The Da do? Up to the counter, knocks on it, knock, knock, knock. Big woollyback culchie guard sweating Irish stew into his armpits. What can I do for your honour? Would you ever lock this pup in a cell for the night, says The Da to the copper. I couldn't do that, sir, tis against the regulations. Out to the car, another few punches to the kidney, then home for round two. Good story isn't it? Will I go on? Do you want to hear what happened when I failed the leaving cert? Or maybe Catherine's told you.

Moya Your father never had the chances you had. That was how he was brought up, in a hard world, Johnny. I'd like to have seen you in it for five minutes. It was different then, I can tell you. Times were tough then, and he worked like a dog for you and you never gave him a thought.

Johnny (*shouts*) And what about me? What thought did he fucking give me? Or *you*, when it fucking mattered?

Moya *gets up and leaves the room.* **Johnny** *lights a cigarette.*

Medbh Thanks very much, Johnny.

Johnny What?

Catherine Can't you just have a bit of respect for him? For once in your life can you have respect for something?

Johnny Respect. Beautiful.

Catherine He was her husband, for Christ's sake. He was your father.

Johnny He was a cold vicious bastard and you know it.

Medbh Don't say that, Johnny.

Johnny Oh the dutiful daughter. What about you and your man?

Medbh Me and who?

Johnny You know, that fucking long streak of misery who knocked you up and then disappeared. Luke the fucking fluke. A little grandson to dandle on his knee. You weren't so complimentary about the old man back in those days.

Medbh Daddy didn't understand the situation, that's all.

Johnny Oh, he understood the situation.

Medbh He didn't.

Johnny   He understood when he found out what happened to it all right. He understood when he found out that junior wouldn't be arriving after all.

Catherine   Johnny, for God's sake.

Medbh   I don't want to talk about that now.

Johnny   You broke his watery excuse for a heart when you did that. So don't throw stones, Medbh. Glass houses and all that.

Medbh   You've a fucking neck on you calling him cold. He wasn't as cold as you when you feel like it.

Johnny   Oh, he was cold all right. Yes. He was cold. And what hurts her over there, what drives dear Catherine absolutely crazy, what makes her rip her fucking headlights out and dance on them is that I loved him anyway. And she was his pet, and she didn't. And she just can't figure that out.

Catherine   Don't you say that. I loved him too.

Johnny   Oh yeah, you did all right. And that's why nobody's here today, I suppose? Look at you. You wouldn't know anything about that, would you? Well anyway, he beat the shit out of me, Tom, when I was bad, and I loved him anway, and I think he was right. And when he was beating the shit out of me I knew it was his sick fuck way of telling me he loved me, the poor bastard, and when I have kids I'm going to beat the shit out of them too in his memory. In fact, it's the only reason I'm going to have kids.

Catherine *is now in tears again.*

Tom   That's enough, Johnny, for God's sake.

Catherine   I loved him too. I loved him too!

Johnny   What would you know about love?

Catherine   As much as you anyway.

Johnny   My Jesus, you're in trouble then.

Catherine   What the hell is the matter with you? Do you have to do this?

Johnny   Oh no, I don't have to. But it fills in the time. While we're waiting for all the special guests to arrive.

Catherine   I loved him. At least I told him I loved him.

Johnny   Oh great. Divvy out the medals. Call the President. Mrs Robinson? Are you there?!!

Catherine   Did you ever tell him?

Johnny   Don't make me puke.

Catherine   Did you ever tell him you loved him in your life?

Johnny   Daddy, Daddy, I wuv you. You told him that to embarrass him. You told him that because you fucking hated him.

Medbh   She did not. Don't say that about her.

Johnny   Sisterly solidarity, Tom. I'm sure you've read about it in *Cosmopolitan* while you're waiting for the dentist. And here it is in real life.

Catherine   I was very fond of dad.

Johnny   He embarrassed the shit out of you and you know it.

Catherine   He did not.

Johnny   When did you ever have a friend in the house when he was here? He embarrassed you, and that shower of middle-class cunts you call friends. My Christ, Catherine and her friends. I used to come home from school and find a load of them sitting around perming each other's hair and listening to Wham, and if you shouted Fiona in here you would've been trampled to death in the stampede.

Medbh   And you're the humble proletariat I suppose.

Johnny   Oh, I'm not saying that now, Joxer. I leave that to you and your revolutionary thespian mates. Medbh studied acting, you see, Tom, in Trinity College, Dublin. She and her little pals used to put on plays in some basement on the Northside. For the working class, you know. God now, they really had the bourgeoisie shaking in their shoes.

Medbh   There's nothing more middle class than using middle class as an insult. You might learn that one day.

Johnny   My Christ, listen to Forrest Gump over there. Get that out of the fucking Christmas cracker, did you?

Catherine   You shagged off to London first chance you got and started shoving coke up your nose just to teach him a lesson. That's how much you loved him.

Johnny   And you're a total stranger to the prohibited substance, of course, aren't you? Look at you. Last time I saw you you were developing a third nostril. How much of it did you bring in with you this time? You didn't know that, did you, Tom? Last time she was here, last Christmas, she brought half a pound of Colombian nose candy home from the Big Apple with her, just to help her over the festive season. Her fucking handbag was like Diego Maradonna's. Not that I blame her, of course. I mean I am a great believer in Einstein's theory of relativity myself, of course – time goes a lot more fucking slowly when you're with your relatives, but still, but still. A white Christmas is certainly what Catherine had. But you wouldn't know about that.

Tom   I do know about that.

Johnny   Oh do you?

Tom   We've talked about it. I know about it. I think your sister's a very brave person. For trying to deal with her problems. Instead of boring everyone to death about them.

Medbh   So do I.

Johnny   Oh you've talked about it. How fucking nineties. Sure, get it out, Catherine. We'll all have some. I'm sure you've brought another big bag of it.

Tom *goes to lunge at* **Johnny**. **Catherine** *grabs his wrist.*

Tom You've some mouth on you, Johnny. You'll get yourself in a lot of trouble one day.

Johnny Oh bejayzus, the rattling boy from the bog is going to teach me a lesson.

Tom It's a pity nobody ever did.

Catherine Leave it, Tom. He's only trying to annoy me.

Johnny If I was trying to annoy you, you'd be fucking annoyed, dear. And you'd stay annoyed.

Catherine Big man, aren't you? When you're drunk.

Johnny I know you anyway. I can press your buttons any time I like, honey, and don't you ever forget that.

Medbh Shut the fuck up, the two of you. Ma's coming.

Moya *comes in wearing a dressing-gown over her clothes.*

Moya I thought I heard the door. Is anyone here?

Johnny No, Ma. Nobody's here. Yet.

Medbh Just us, Ma.

Johnny But you never know who might turn up later, of course. Do you, Catherine?

Moya Is everything all right? Have you been crying, Catherine, love?

Catherine No.

Johnny Nobody's crying, Ma. Everything's great. Just shooting the breeze, you know. Just chewing the old familial fat. And there's plenty of it here to chew, God knows.

He gets up and goes to the window.

Oh, there'll be plenty here to chew, Joxer. Plenty here to chew.

Lights out.

Act Three

Lights up on the living-room. **Tom**, **Medbh** *and* **Johnny** *are sitting in the middle of the room as before, smoking and drinking.* **Catherine** *is sitting away from the group looking moody.*

Tom *and* **Medbh** *are singing together.*

Tom *and* **Medbh**
  Well if I was a small bird and had wings that could fly
  I would fly o'er the sea where my true love does lie
  Seven years and six months since he left this bright shore
  He's my bonny light horseman who I'll never see more.

As the song ends, **Johnny** *claps and whistles.*

Enter **Moya** *from the street. She looks at her watch.*

Moya   It's after seven already. And no sign of a soul.

Johnny   Don't worry about it, Ma. Aren't we all here? And aren't we singing?

Moya   But God, it's getting late, though. Where do you think they are?

Catherine   Stop worrying, Mum.

Moya   I can't figure it out though. I thought there'd be gangs here by now.

Medbh *and* **Catherine** *avoid* **Johnny**'s *glance.*

Johnny   Me too. Me too. But you never know. It's never too late. So what'll we do now? Will we have another song?

Catherine   I think we've had enough singing actually.

Johnny   But sure isn't there always supposed to be singing at a good auld Dubbalin wake?

Catherine   God stop, will you. You sound like one of the fucking Furey Brothers.

Medbh   You know, Catherine, I sometimes think you walk around with a fucking corn cob up your arse. If you sang a bit yourself it might loosen you up a bit.

Catherine   I do sing, when I want to.

Medbh   Well, I've never heard you.

Catherine   Well, I do. What would you know about me anyway?

Medbh   I've never heard you singing, that's all I'm saying.

Moya   Catherine always used to sing when she was a girl. She'd a lovely little voice, Tom. Enda always said that. And he loved singing himself, of course. He loved all the old Wexford rebel songs.

Johnny   Oh yes, of course. The Sunday drive into the country, Tom. That's when Catherine used to sing. We'd all get into the car and like everyone else in Dublin we'd drive out to the Sally Gap, because that's what The Da thought we should do of a Sundah. We'd set off after the lunch, in a convoy of five thousand cars, every car in Dublin, all full of mammies and daddies and little kids smacked out of their head on the angel dust in the roast beef. All out to have a look at the country dwellers, the woollybacks of the County Wickla. And when we got there, there'd be three million bewildered suburbanites all lined up and staring into the Sally Gap like they were waiting for the second fucking coming or something. And then Catherine would sing on the way home.

Catherine   Well, I don't want to sing now.

Medbh   Don't be so stubborn. Just sing, for fuck's sake.

Catherine   I don't want to, I said.

Medbh   All right, don't then, Jesus.

Moya   Oh stop it, the pair of you. You're like a couple of fishwives.

Johnny   Will you have a drink, Ma?

Moya   What? Oh, I suppose I might have a small whiskey.

Johnny   Oh, a ball of malt there me auld scout, for the mother of all the Behans.

Medbh *pours drinks.*

Medbh   Do you want something to eat, Ma?

Moya   No no. I wouldn't be able.

Johnny (*to* **Moya**)   Sit down here beside me, Ma.

Moya *sits beside him.* **Johnny** *kisses her on the cheek.*

Johnny   I'm sorry for rowing with you earlier.

Moya (*with sarcasm*)   I'm sure you are. You look fierce sorry all right.

Johnny *grabs her hand and swings it while he sings.*

Johnny (*singing*)
   Ah sure, Dubbalin can be heaven
   With a coffee at eleven
   And a strowill in Steven's Green.
   There's no need to worry
   There's no need to hurry
   You're a king and your lady's a queen.

Moya *pulls her hand away, laughing.*

Moya   Stop will you. You're as odd as two left feet, you are.

Medbh   Are you all right, now, Ma?

Moya   I'm grand, love. I'm tired that's all. I haven't slept the last few nights. I've been having strange dreams.

Catherine   Have you been dreaming about daddy?

Moya   No, love. I don't think so. It was just a funny dream. I dreamed I was in a house somewhere, a house that I knew. It was a big old house with paintings on the walls. And I was walking around on my own. There was a child's laughter coming from one of the rooms. But the house was so big I couldn't find where it was coming from.

Johnny   That'll be tuna.

Moya   What?

Johnny   Tuna sandwiches. They always give me strange dreams too, I don't know what it is about tuna, but it always gives me strange dreams. Does it give you strange dreams, Tom?

Tom   No, it doesn't.

Johnny   Whaddyamean, no?

Tom   Well, I don't like tuna.

Johnny   Well, no wonder you don't have dreams then.

Tom   I have dreams all right.

Johnny   Do you dream about Catherine, eh?

Tom   I did dream about her once.

Johnny   Oh God, tell us. Wait now till I get another drink. Give us a whiskey there, darling.

Catherine *pours him one.*

Johnny   Ah, give us a bit more, will you?

Catherine *pours him out more. He takes the bottle from her and fills his glass. She makes drinks for everyone else.*

Tom   You don't want to hear.

Johnny   I do, Tom. Tell me.

Moya   Sure, tell us, Tom.

Tom   Well, I was walking by the sea. It was down near home. And it seemed to be early in the morning. There was nobody around. It was just me, by myself, and I could hear the seagulls. And the sound of the waves on the beach. And suddenly, I saw her about twenty feet away from me out in the sea. Catherine. Up to her waist in the water. You were calling out to me, and I went to try to get to you. And I couldn't. I kept walking through the water. And running then. But the more I ran, the further away from me you were.

Johnny   That's it?

Tom   That's it. She was up to her waist in the water.

Catherine   I wonder what that could mean.

Moya   It sounds very deep.

Tom   What? The water?

Moya   No love. I mean it sounds very . . . it sounds spiritual or something. Would that be the word?

Johnny   You were probably pissing. She used to do that, you know, when we were children. She used to piss in the sea and in swimming pools. It was ferocious.

Catherine (*laughing*)   I did not.

Johnny   She did. It was too too embarrassing. And she crapped in a swimming pool once. In Leisureland, in Galway.

Catherine   I did not, you little fucker.

Moya   Catherine. Language, please.

Catherine   I didn't though.

Moya   Sure don't mind that galoot. I know well you didn't.

Johnny   She did. There we were, Tom, in the pool in Leisureland, down in your part of the world, playing, you know, trying to drown the bejayzus out of each other, and all of a sudden her face goes all funny, and out it comes. This big turd, you know, like the battleship Potempkin. Floating up to the top. Jesus Christ, I couldn't believe it.

Catherine   And what about you that summer? We were in the Gaeltacht, and he got off with this big lump from the Northside. She was six foot tall and ugly as sin, with a big brace on her teeth. She had a head on her like a giraffe. And when he got off with her he got his tongue stuck in the brace. I could hear him screaming. And I ran into the room and there he was. And Bean Ui Costello ran in, roaring and shouting at us not to be speaking English. And he was hopping around, trying to get his tongue out.

Johnny   My eyes still water whenever I hear Irish spoken, Tom. People sometimes think it's national pride.

Moya   My God now, I never knew any of this. There we were thinking it would help your education.

Catherine   Oh it did, Mother.

Johnny   And do you remember that time with the duck?

Medbh   What time was that?

Johnny   Catherine there, she found this duck.

Catherine   I did not. What are you talking about?

Johnny   You found a duck. Don't you remember?

Catherine   I don't know. Do I?

Johnny   She found this duck you see, Tom, just wandering down the street in Spiddal. We were down in Spiddal with The Da, staying in the little hotel, and she brought it back to the hotel and into the bar she goes with the duck under her arm. And the barman says, Jesus Christ, where did you get that ugly looking pig? And Catherine says, what do you mean? That's not a pig. And the barman says, no, I was talking to the duck.

Catherine   Ha bloody ha.

Moya   Aren't dreams funny though? The things we keep hidden away, you know. I remember saying that to Enda, about all the old rubbish he had in the study. And he said, it's like your dreams, Moya. Everything is filed away somewhere and you never know when it's going to come out.

Johnny   Good old Pops. Zen as ever. The Maharishi of Usher's Quay.

Tom   It kind of bothered me though, that dream. I didn't know what it was about. And I woke up in a sweat over it.

Johnny   And sweat, of course, by its very nature, is salty.

Moya   God, it's a strange one all right. That'd give you the willies.

Johnny   Cheese.

Tom   What?

Johnny   Cheese gives you scary dreams, or erotic dreams, one or the other. That's what I find anyway.

Catherine *clicks her tongue and gets up. She goes to the window and looks out.*

Johnny   It's gospel. I always find Camembert is the best thing for erotic dreams, I don't know why. It's the smell of soft French feet I suppose.

Moya   Listen to him. I'll put my soft French foot in your backside in a minute, you scut.

Catherine   The garden's a bit of a mess, Mum, isn't it?

Moya   Well, with Enda being sick, love. We've let it go to pot a bit. Enda always took a great pride in his garden, Tom. He always loved it. He never had a garden as a boy, you see. Not that I did either, God knows. And when we moved in here it was his pride and joy. He was happy as Larry out there, with his garden, just doing the grass. And he used to go down to the garage every Saturday with one of the kids, when they were young. With Johnny usually, and they'd bring the can, you know, for petrol. For the lawnmower. And it was the kind of a garage where they sold different things. It was old-fashioned. They sold messages, you know, and flowers too. And he'd buy me roses. Red roses every Saturday. Do you remember that, Johnny?

Johnny   Yeah. I remember they didn't have them one week and he nearly threw the head.

Moya   And then when the kids had grown up, we'd just go down together sometimes. Enda and myself, every Saturday, like a couple of old duffers. And Mr Clancy down in the garage got to know us over the years. Red roses, Mister Doyle, he'd say, and a can of petrol. A funny combination, isn't it?

Silence.

Tom   And how did you meet your husband, Moya? If you don't mind me asking.

Moya   God, love, it's so long ago I nearly don't remember.

Medbh She does so remember, don't mind her. It was at a dance, wasn't it?

Moya No it wasn't actually, if you're so smart.

Medbh How was it, then?

Moya I was over in London, Tom, in digs, you know. God it was thirty years ago. I was in a little play over there. *Juno and the Paycock* by O'Casey. And it was only a small part now, I was Mary, the daughter, even though this shower call me Juno sometimes, for slagging. But it was marvellous to be in London, Tom. And I lived with this nice little Jewish family in Hammersmith, lovely people they were. There were dances back then, in the Hammersmith Palais. Oh God, there'd be great dances there. All the Irish would go on a certain night, do you know? It was a kind of home away from home.

Tom And you met him there?

Moya Well, no. What happened was that Enda and his pal went along one night. To the dance. And they met some girls, and they danced the night away I suppose. And he arranged to meet them the next morning and drive down to Bournemouth. He had some sort of a car, God knows how he got it, and he wanted to go off down to Bournemouth with these girls.

Johnny Bournemouth, you know. The Da was a flash old bastard, wasn't he?

Moya And anyway, next morning he's asleep in the digs. And next thing he knew his pal was waking him up, going, you promised we'd take those two young ones to Bournemouth today. But when they turned up to collect the two ladyfriends, wasn't the one Enda had his eye on not there. She was sick or something, so she'd sent along her friend in her place. And her friend was an awful-looking moose apparently.

Catherine Mother!

Moya   Well, she was. That's what I was told anyway. So
didn't Enda decide he didn't want to go after all. And there I
was walking down the Fulham Palace Road, just minding my
own business and he came up to me. He pulled up beside me
in the car and asked me the time, as bold as you please. He
had a Dublin accent, and so I asked him where he was from.
He was from Usher's Quay and I was from Bride Street, in
the Liberties. He lived about ten minutes from me at home,
imagine. But if I hadn't gone to England I never would've
met him. You wouldn't do it now. Get into a car with a
strange man. But he had a very kind look about him.

Medbh   And what happened so?

Moya   We went to Bournemouth for the day. I remember
everything about it. All the way down in the car he sang
some stupid song that would have been in the hit parade at
the time. It might have been Frank Sinatra. Or Elvis. Yes.
Because Elvis was going then. Elvis was . . . And then we
had a walk down the pier, and then we had our lunch in a
restaurant called English. I remember that because it seemed
so funny to me, that there'd be a restaurant called that, when
I didn't know a restaurant called Irish. Anyway, we talked
for so long that they had to ask us to go, and they putting the
chairs up on top of the tables. And oh, he made me laugh so
much. He was a great joke-teller. He'd have you in stitches.
We walked along the seafront afterwards. And we bought
rock. And Enda told me he'd read in some book that people
were like those sticks of rock, and that if you were to cut
them open, you'd see their . . . nature I suppose . . . written
all the way through them. And God, I thought that was the
maddest thing I'd ever heard in my life. And then we went to
mass at teatime.

Catherine   You went to mass on your date?

Moya   We certainly did. God, we wouldn't miss mass. Not
for Elvis himself.

Johnny   Mass is something we papists have, Tom.

Tom   I know what mass is, thanks.

Catherine (*pointedly*)   He knows what mass is because he was at one today.

Medbh   And what happened then?

Moya   What do you mean?

Medbh   On the way home? Did he get the tongue in?

Moya   Stop that. He was such a gentleman. He dropped me off home at the digs and he said – I'll always remember – 'Moya, I must say, I've had a very pleasant afternoon and I'd be disappointed now if I couldn't see you again.'

Johnny   A great way with the words, all the same.

Moya   So I said I'd see him the next week at the dance. In the Palais. I went with my pal and he came with his. And we danced away the two of us. We got on great. And then, just, the weeks went past. Well, one week then, he asked me if I wanted to meet him beforehand. That was the big thing. That was when you knew you were going together, when you'd meet the fellow outside and he'd pay you in. And we just clicked really. And when the play was over then, I didn't come home to Dublin. And I stayed over there. I got a little job, you know, in a hotel in Earls Court. And he worked in a bookshop on the Charing Cross Road. And the times we had then in London.

Catherine   And did you love him straight away, Mum? When you met him, I mean?

Moya   God, pet, I don't know. I liked him as soon as I met him I suppose. And then before I knew it . . . Well, I remember we had a little row once, and I came on home to Dublin on the boat. And my mother asked me, do you love him, Moya? And I thought, to say I loved him would be like saying . . . like saying that it was rainy today. So I went back to him.

Moya *fights back tears.*

Tom   That's a lovely story, Moya.

Moya   That's the way it was. I loved the children's father and he loved me. We had our ups and downs over the years, of course. But that's the way it was in those days. It wasn't something you thought about. Some people now, they want moonlight and roses the whole time . . .

Catherine   It wasn't always like that though, was it?

Moya   Well, no. But that isn't something that needs to be discussed.

Catherine   But you know that time when you had all the rows . . .

Moya   Catherine, please, not today love.

Catherine   God, I'm just saying, there were rows weren't there? I remember you not getting on well sometimes. That's all I'm saying.

Moya   But sure, every marriage is like that, pet. You'll see when you're married yourself. Please God. Every marriage . . . It's such a very hard thing to get to know a person. My God, you're young, you're beguiled. And then you change. And everything in your life changes. You're not the same people any more. You think love is the feeling in your tummy. That lovely warm feeling when you're falling through the air. But it isn't.

Medbh   So what is it?

Moya   It's when . . . it's when you start to think another person is real.

Catherine   (*laughs*)   I don't know what you mean.

Moya *takes her hand.*

Moya   No. Well, you will, pet, please God. You know sometimes when I think about all of you, Johnny and your sister too, I see myself at your age. Isn't that funny? And I remember all the hopes I had. All that hope is a great thing. You should make the most of it. Because it won't always be like that.

Medbh   Deep, Ma.

Moya   *You* know exactly what I mean though. You all do.

Medbh   I know. I do.

Moya   (*looking at her watch*)   So now. God, it's so late. And I'm talking too much. As usual, says you. I think I'll go in and make us all a nice pot of tea.

She stands and goes to leave.

Tom, your glass is empty there. Go and make another one for yourself, for God's sake. You needn't stand on ceremony here.

Tom   Thanks, Moya.

Moya *goes to leave. Silence in the room.* **Tom** *makes his drink and goes to the window. He peers out.*

Tom   Well, it's another terrible night out there anyway.

Medbh   Is it?

Tom   My God, you wouldn't send a dog out in it.

Silence. After a moment, **Medbh** *makes an effort.*

Medbh   The weather's been fucking poxy this year, Tom. I've never seen anything like it.

Silence.

It's funny. Because I was just thinking: I remember dad saying to us when we were kids. Saint Patrick used to pray that Ireland would sink into the sea with the rains seven years before the world ended. I think it must be happening.

Johnny   No great bloody loss.

Tom   Well, funny enough, I was only just saying to that girl in the church today, I can never remember the weather being so bad. When I lived in Ireland, I mean. I mean, yes, you'd have your hard winters, but now half the bloody country's flooded, she was saying. All the farmers down the west are up in arms about it.

Medbh   Yeah, so they are, I believe. Which girl was that?

Tom   Oh, just . . . that girl, you know.

Medbh   Which?

Tom   That one your father knew.

Catherine *turns and glares at him.*

Catherine   You mean, you spoke to her?

Tom (*laughs*)   Well, I just said hello, Catherine. It was after the mass when you were talking to everybody, and I just slipped out for a fag. And she was there by herself, and the girl was upset. I mean, I had to just say nod and say hello.

Catherine   You're joking me.

Tom (*laughs nervously*)   What, Catherine? I only gave her the time of day, for God's sake. Sure, I only said hello and goodbye to the girl, that's all.

Moya *suddenly comes in with a tea tray.*

Moya   Which girl was that, Tom?

Tom   I . . . nobody, Moya. Just this girl who was at the funeral.

Moya (*laughing, to* **Catherine**)   You'll have to be up early in the morning to keep tags on this fellow anyway, love. He's an eye for the ladies I see. Tell us, was she good-looking, Tom?

Tom   Well, I was only talking to her for a second.

Catherine *stands suddenly and goes to the window.*

Moya   Oh God, would you look? There's going to be a big lovers' tiff now. She wants you on a short leash anyhow, Tom.

Catherine   Tom does and says exactly what he likes.

Tom   I do not, Catherine.

Catherine   Oh, you do all right.

Tom   I said I'm sorry, Catherine. Don't be embarrassing me now, in front of everyone.

Silence for some moments.

Moya   My God, Catherine, stop. Look at the puss on you. What's ailing you, darling? The poor fellow was only being polite, for heaven's sake. There's no harm in that. Tell us, who was she anyway, Tom?

Tom   I don't know who she was.

Moya   Well, what did she look like then?

Tom   I didn't really see.

Moya (*laughs*)   Sure you must have. Go on, tell us. I won't say a word.

Tom   I . . . I think she might have a had a mark on her face.

Medbh   I don't think I saw anyone like that.

Silence. **Moya** *sips her drink.*

Tom   Well, I just said hello, that's all. She seemed to be so upset, and I only . . . Would you not come back and sit down, Catherine?

Moya (*laughs, a little too loudly*)   Do you know, now that you mention it, I think I saw you. A girl in her twenties, maybe. Yes. With the birthmark? Sure I saw you myself in the porch, he was just chatting, dear. I know all about her actually. Tom was only being mannerly, weren't you, Tom?

Tom (*to* **Catherine**)   Will you not sit down, love?

Moya   She's just some girl from the college, Tom. Daddy was helping her out with her studies. She was falling behind, and he was giving her a dig out. With advice, you know. On books. Enda was such a generous person, you know, Tom. Oh, he had so much knowledge, but he was generous about it too. He got on great with all the students.

She takes another sip of her drink.

Enda was always very popular. Very good with people. Always very . . .

Catherine   Mum, for God's sake.

Moya (*laughs*)   What?

Medbh   Leave it, Catherine.

Catherine   What difference does it make now? Why can't we all just tell the truth?

Moya   What do you mean, love?

Medbh   She doesn't mean anything.

Tom   Catherine, please, I'm sorry if I've done anything I shouldn't.

Moya   Don't be silly, Tom, you've done nothing bad at all, love. She's some girl who daddy was helping out with her studies. It's very simple. She's from Darndale. Now, sit down there and we'll have a cup of tea together and not be rowing.

Catherine   Stop this!

Moya   Stop what, love?

Catherine *reaches into her pocket and takes out the photograph she removed from the book the day before.*

Catherine   What's that?

Moya *takes the photo, looks at it for a few moments.*

Moya   It's a photograph. So what?

Catherine   It's a photograph of her, Mum. Of that girl. It was in a book over there on the shelf.

Moya   Well, isn't that nice? Is it a crime to have a photograph of a person now?

Catherine *snaps it out of her hand.*

Catherine   Are you blind? (*She turns it over and reads aloud.*) 'To Enda, with all my love and thanks, from Helen.'

Moya   Well, what does that mean?

Catherine   Don't you really know what it means? Don't tell me you don't, Mum. I don't believe it. You lived with the man for thirty years, you must know.

Moya (*laughs*)   What?

Catherine   You know well. Don't laugh at me, you do know. That's why nobody's here, Mum. You must know that. It was all over UCD when I was there. It was the laugh of the whole place. Big big joke. Big laughs all round. And when Medbh was there too, before she left. That's *why* she left, Mum. Because she had to, with all the talk.

Medbh   I did not, Catherine.

Catherine   That's not what you told *me*. It is so and you know it. People used to laugh about it, Mum. Everyone in the place laughed about it. Why do you think nobody's here?

Moya   God, I haven't a clue. Wasn't I only just saying that.

Catherine   How would anyone come here? When they've no idea what might happen today? When they've no idea what bloody scene they might fucking see if she turned up here?

Moya   You'd want to calm down now, my girl. You're losing the run of yourself, isn't she, Tom?

Catherine   Don't tell me to calm down! Do you know what it was like for us? They'd point at us and they'd laugh when we were passing by in the corridors . . .

Moya   Stop it, I said.

Catherine   'There's Enda Doyle's daughters, oh, you know the story on him and your one, don't you? Been going on for years now. Do you think the wife knows? Does she just pretend not to know, do you think?' What do you think that was like for us?

Moya   Things were good for you. Good for you always. We worked bloody hard enough so they would be. And this is the thanks . . .

Catherine   Good for us? Good for us? When your father is fucking the arse off some little tart who's young enough . . .

Moya *lashes out and slaps her in the face.*

Moya   You little bloody bitch! How dare you! That's a terrible thing to say about your father. If you knew the love he had for this family, the sacrifices, the trouble he went to.

Catherine *starts to cry.*

Moya   Do you know what it was like for him? When he was your age he'd been working fifteen years. There's not one of you kids now would know the meaning of responsibility. Perfection is what you want. The world handed up to you on a bloody plate. Nothing else will damn well do you, and then you blame everyone else for everything.

Catherine *runs out in tears.* **Medbh** *runs after her.*

Johnny   Ma . . .

Moya   My God Almighty, there's lovely talk for you now.

Tom   Moya. Look, I didn't . . . I mean I really . . .

Moya   I'm sorry now, Tom, that you've been embarrassed. I don't know what must have come over her. I just don't know. I think we're all a bit tired, that's all, and I don't mind people having a drink, but I won't have that kind of talk.

Johnny *goes and puts his arm around her shoulder.*

Johnny   Relax, Ma.

Moya   I'm perfectly relaxed, thank you. But I'm damned if I'll have that knacker-talk in the house though. The bloody cheek of her.

Silence. **Moya** *looks at her watch.*

Moya   I'll think I'll just go out to the road again, and see if anybody's coming.

Johnny   Leave it, Ma. Sure nobody's coming now.

Moya   You don't know that. They might be here any minute.

Johnny   Ma, it's lashing rain out there. Go on up and have a rest and if anyone comes I'll call you.

Moya   Well, I'm sorry now if I've embarrassed anybody. I'm sorry if I made a fool of myself.

Johnny   You haven't, Ma.

Moya   But we didn't do everything we did, your father and me, to have that kind of filthy knacker's talk in the house.

Johnny   I know, Ma.

Moya   We did not. There's no need for that kind of filthy talk. You wouldn't hear it in a whorehouse.

Tom   Moya, I'm sure Catherine didn't mean any harm.

Moya   Tom, you're very welcome here, but I'll thank you not to hand me out lectures on my own family if you please!

Moya *leaves the room.*

Tom *puts his head in his hands.*

Tom   Jesus.

Johnny   So. Do Protestants have mothers, Tom?

Tom   You're very smart, aren't you?

Johnny   Not as smart as you, pal. We've all just seen how fucking smart you are.

Tom *stands and goes to leave.*

Johnny   Listen, stay and have a drink, why don't you. It's done now.

Tom   I'm tired. And I've had enough drink.

Johnny   Well, look, I'm sorry for having a go at you, all right? I get a bit puerile sometimes, my psychiatrist says. I suffer from depression, you know. But I'm puerile too, he tells me. Fifty quid a session and I'm puerile. Look it up in the dictionary, Tom.

Tom   No it's OK, Johnny. I got my leaving cert, you know?

Johnny (*laughs softly*)   Good man.

Tom *leaves.* **Johnny** *swigs from his glass. Distant sound of an argument upstairs. Muffled shouting, slamming doors.*

After a moment **Johnny** *gets up, goes to the television, inserts a video tape and presses play. His father's image appears on the screen.* **Johnny** *raises his glass in mock salute.*

Johnny   Look at me, Da. I'm on top of the world.

Enda   . . . And the fields were laid out like bedspreads or something, as far as the eye could see, all the way down to Galway Bay. There were birds too, great big cormorants I suppose, that you get down there in that part of the world. And we stopped in Spiddal, for our tea. It was quite cold and there was that lovely smell in the air, of turf, and the salty tang of the sea. Mass was on in the church and you could hear the choir singing. And the people in the shops were all talking in Irish. It was such a lovely sound to hear, the sound of people all talking in Irish. And Moya asked me to say a poem for her.

Suddenly, **Medbh** *runs through the room in tears and grabs her coat.* **Johnny** *presses pause on the remote.*

Johnny   Medbh!

Medbh *runs out into the rain.* **Johnny** *looks at the screen.*

Johnny   You're missing a really fun day, Da. Do you know that? And isn't it just like you to cause all the trouble and then not be here, isn't it? Do you know what I'd really like now, Da? A big load of coke. That's what I'd like. A big fucking pillow-case full of it.

Johnny *presses play again.*

Enda   And we stayed out in Barna. And the way they had the food then if they ran out of plates was that it was all put out on the table. There'd be a big mound of new potatoes all swimming in butter . . .

Johnny *presses the pause button, freezing his father's face.*

Johnny   What do you think, Da? Do you think that sister of mine's brought anything over with her, do you? Help her through the stress? Will we take a look, Da?

He begins rummaging through **Catherine***'s handbag. He pulls various items out of it and scatters them around. He finds the envelope containing his father's ashes. He opens it.*

Johnny (*laughing*)   I knew it. I fucking knew it.

He takes the envelope to the table and spreads the ashes out into lines on a plate.

I knew my big sister wouldn't let me down, Da.

He grabs a mass card and tears off a piece of paper. He rolls it up and snorts one of the lines of ashes. He stares at his father's face on the screen.

Well, Da, you know now. You know if there's anything up there now. You always wondered, didn't you? You said you knew for sure, but you always wondered. I knew that. You wanted everything to be sure. And you wanted everyone to be sure about you. But they weren't. Because you had your little secrets, didn't you, Da? Oh, you had your secrets all right.

He brings a can of beer with him, sits down on the floor and presses the play button.

Enda   And then one day, didn't we all drive up to Cleggan and got the ferry out to Innishboffin, Moya and the girls, and the young lad, and the sea was so . . . the colour of amethysts, it was, and so clear and cold when you put your hand in the water. And we came out to the island and looked at Grace O'Malley's castle, and I told the young lad all about her. Grace O'Malley, the pirate queen, and I thought then, as I looked at it, of a line I once read somewhere . . .

Johnny *presses pause button.*

Johnny   Remember that time I asked you if God was really there, do you? You poor old bastard. That time down in Connemara. It was late at night and we were walking up the boreen. It was pitch black and I had my hand in your hand. And we had torches, the two of us. You were smoking your pipe and when I shone my torch on your face you were smiling. And I asked you why. And you told me you were just happy. Happy. And I asked you why. And you said you were just happy to be here with your son. And we walked on a bit, and then I said to you, Daddy, is God just like Santa Claus? . . . And then you weren't happy any more, were you, Da? You weren't happy then. I'm so ashamed of you now, Johnny, you said. You've spoiled everything now. I'm so ashamed of you now for saying that.

He sits back, watches the screen, presses the remote and plays the video tape again.

Enda   . . . And when Alexander saw the breadth of his domain, he wept, for there were no more worlds to conquer . . .

Johnny   Enda Michael Malachi Doyle. You poor old fucking phoney.

He pauses the screen again. He begins to sing softly.

As I was climbing the scaffold high
My own dear father was standing by
But my own dear father did me deny.
And the name he gave me
Was The Croppy Boy.

Lights fade. Sound of waves breaking on a shore.

Enter **Young Enda** *and* **Young Moya**, *hand in hand.* **Young Moya** *is in gloomy mood.*

Young Enda   The sea looks beautiful tonight, Moya, doesn't it?

Young Moya   It looks the same as it always does.

Young Enda   But look at the lights out there, the way they move on the water. That's France over there, you know. And look at the moon up there.

Young Moya   I think the moon is looking for lovers.

Young Enda   My God, that's ripe talk, if your mother heard it.

Young Moya   It's in a play, you fool. It's in *Salome*, by Oscar Wilde.

Young Enda   Is it now? Well, come here and give us a kiss then, Salome. Before I lose my head over you.

Young Moya *dodges his advance, with genuine irritation.*

Young Moya   Stop, would you. I'm not in the mood.

Young Enda   You're in cranky humour tonight.

Young Moya   Don't be saying that.

Young Enda *laughs softly.*

Young Moya   What's so funny all of a sudden?

Young Enda   Nothing, nothing. 'But why did I laugh tonight?' That's in a poem by John Keats.

Young Moya   God, Enda, all your talk of books and poems. And what do you know about anything? For all your books?

Young Enda *is a little shocked. But he laughs gently again and takes her hand.*

Young Enda   Nothing. I know nothing at all. And I don't care. I'll burn my books!

Young Moya *softens, in spite of herself.*

Young Moya   That'll be the day all right. You're mad about those stupid old books of yours.

Young Enda   Will we get married, Moya?

Young Moya's *demeanour changes again. She turns away.*

Young Moya   God, you're very serious aren't you.

Young Enda   We could go home to Ireland.

Young Moya (*laughs dismissively*)   How could we do that?

Young Enda   We could try, couldn't we?

Young Moya   That's only dreaming, Enda. There's nothing at home now, you know that.

Young Enda   That's not true, love. There's plenty of opportunity at home these days. I was only reading in the paper the other day, where they said that. The new government at home.

Young Moya   They say more than their prayers, that shower of gombeen counter jumpers. If there's so much bloody opportunity what's everyone doing over here?

Young Enda   But things are changing at home now, Moya. That's what everyone says. They're building houses, left, right and centre. Things are on the up now. They're building everything up. I read about this job a while ago, in the university in Dublin. Junior Librarian. I thought it'd be a handy enough sit if I could get it. And I did the interview when I was at home over Christmas. And guess what?

Young Moya   What?

Young Enda   I got it, Moya. I'm after getting it. We can get married now, and go home to Ireland.

Young Moya   You've everything figured out, haven't you?

Young Enda   I love you, Moya.

Young Moya   You say you love me and you don't even talk to me about something like that. How do you know that's what I want to do? Did that ever dawn on you for a minute?

Young Enda   God, I'm sorry, Moya. I thought I'd surprise you. I thought it was what you wanted.

Young Moya   Oh did you now? You're bloody clairvoyant as well are you?

Young Enda   I'm sorry, Moya. You know I do love you.

Silence.

Young Moya   Well, you know I'm fond of you as well. God help me.

She turns to him. He kisses her.

Young Enda   We could be happy as anything together, you know, over at home where we belong. And I'm so fond of you, Moya. I really am.

Young Moya   I know you are.

Young Enda   If I've let you down some way . . .

Young Moya   You haven't let me down. I just . . .

She hugs him.

Don't ever leave me, Enda, sure you wouldn't?

Young Enda   How would I leave you? Haven't I just asked you to marry me?

Young Moya   Please don't ever leave me though.

Thunder rumbles.

Young Enda   Come on, love. We'll catch our deaths.

Lights fade to darkness as **Young Enda** *and* **Young Moya** *run off. Sound of thunder continues.*

Act Four

Lights up on the living-room. It is late at night. Continuing thunder and lightning outside. The sound of heavy rain. **Johnny** *is asleep on the floor behind the couch, so that he cannot be seen from the door. On the frozen video screen,* **Enda**'s *face is distorted into a smile.*

Medbh *comes in from outside, her clothes soaked. She takes off her coat and throws it over a chair. She notices the video and switches it on. She sits on the edge of a chair and watches it for the first few lines. Then as* **Enda**'s *song continues, she stands up, takes off her shoes and socks, her wet shirt and jeans. She takes her father's coat from the hanger and puts it on. Then she goes to the table, which is still full of food. She takes a sandwich and a bottle of beer. Opens the beer. (All this action takes place while* **Enda** *is singing.)*

Enda
  At Boolavogue, as the sun was setting
  O'er the bright May meadows of Shelmalier
  A rebel hand set the heather blazing
  And brought the neighbours from far and near.
  Then Father Murphy from old Kilcormac
  Spurred up the rocks with a warning cry
  Arm, arm! he cried. For I've come to lead you.
  For Ireland's freedom, we'll fight or die.

  He led us on, 'gainst the coming soldiers
  The cowardly yeomen we put to flight
  Down at the Harrow, the boys of Wexford
  Showed England's regiments how men could fight . . .

By now, **Medbh** *is sitting on the floor in front of the video, eating a sandwich and drinking a beer. She presses pause, gets up and turns on a wall lamp, which suffuses the room with dim yellow light.* **Johnny** *wakes up.*

Johnny   Who's there?

Medbh *jumps.*

Medbh   Jesus. Johnny. You scared me.

Johnny   What time is it?

Medbh   It's midnight. Jesus, my heart.

Johnny   Fuck. Midnight, is it? Where were you?

Medbh   I went down to Dooley's to see Charlie Foster.

Johnny   Fuck. Dooley's. What are you going to that kip for?

Medbh   Dooley's is all right.

Johnny   Good Christ. Dooley's. They used to search you for weapons on the way into that place, and if you didn't have any they'd kick the shit out of you.

Medbh   It's good crack down there now. It's changed a good bit since you've been away.

Johnny   And how's Charlie? I heard he was home for a few months.

Medbh   He's grand. I've been seeing a bit of him, you know. Since he's been home from Oz.

Johnny   Which bit of him have you been seeing?

Medbh   Don't slag me, Johnny. Please.

Silence.

Johnny   Is it serious?

Medbh   Ah, I like him all right. I'm a bit gone on him.

Johnny   Well, Charlie's a great bloke.

Medbh   Yeah he is. He's gas.

Johnny   I've a lot of time for Charlie.

Medbh   Yeah. Me too.

Johnny   Well, why do you look like a bulldog sucking piss off a nettle? What's up with you?

Medbh   He asked me to go to Australia with him, Johnny. He asked me to go over with him, to live, you know. He's set up over there. In Melbourne. He wants me to go with him. He's going back next week.

Johnny   Are you going?

Silence.

Medbh   No, I'm not.

Johnny   Why not?

Medbh   I don't really know. But I'm not. I've been thinking about it a lot lately. I've been stringing him along, I suppose. I told him I'd tell him tonight for sure.

Johnny   Go, Medbh. What the hell are you hanging around this dump for?

Medbh   Stop.

Johnny   Christ, Medbh, get on that plane and go. Don't even think about it, just do it. Sure, Charlie's been mad about you since we were kids, you know that.

Medbh   I know, and I'm . . . I don't know if I've got what it takes. To go all that way. I mean, it's Australia, Johnny. It's the other side of the world. And then if it didn't work out.

Johnny   What are you talking about?

Medbh   Who'd look after Ma? Now she's on her own?

Johnny   That's only making excuses, Medbh.

Medbh   Well, would you fucking do it? Would you and Jenny come home to look after her?

Johnny   What about Catherine?

Medbh   She'll never come home now. You know that. Her and Tom are getting married next Christmas. She told me earlier.

Johnny   Has she told ma?

Medbh   She's going to tell her tomorrow. She wanted to wait until after the funeral.

Johnny   Big of her.

Medbh   She's doing so well now, Johnny. Would you not give her a break?

Johnny   I'll give her a compound fucking fracture.

Medbh   It wasn't easy for her, you know. When she went out to New York first she was still in a bad way.

Johnny   Yeah, well, we've all taken a few drugs in our time.

Medbh   Not the way she did, Johnny. You know that. You know what she was like. She was so mixed up about everything. All the rows at home, they hit her very hard. You remember all the rows they had when we were kids. But she's done a lot of work on her head over there.

Johnny   Work on her head. I love it.

Medbh   Well, it's true.

Johnny   I know. Look, I love her like a sister, OK? Just not one of mine.

Medbh   She loves you a lot, you know.

Johnny   She's a funny way of showing it.

Medbh   Well, so do you.

Johnny   I suppose I do. It's a family trait.

Medbh   Do you want a drink?

Johnny   Yeah. I suppose.

Medbh *gets two cans of beer and a pack of cigarettes.*

Medbh   So did anyone come while I was out? From the pub or anything.

Johnny   Don't, Medbh. You know nobody came.

Medbh   Johnny, I . . . How did you know?

Johnny   When I got in this morning the phone was ringing. It was some professor from the college. He wanted to know if it was true we didn't want people coming back to the house. It was a very revealing conversation.

Medbh   It wasn't my idea. Catherine was worried there'd be a scene. If that girl turned up. You're not to throw the head with her, Johnny, please.

Johnny   I'm not, I'm not. Maybe she was right.

Medbh   All the food ma made.

Johnny   She's other things on her mind now, besides food.

Medbh   Do you think it's true, Johnny? About dad and that girl?

Johnny   What does it matter now? Things aren't always what they seem.

Medbh   People did say it, you know. In UCD. You'd see them together all the time too. I remember bumping into them together in the bar once. And he looked right through me.

Johnny   Medbh, let's leave it be.

Moya *comes in, wearing a dressing-gown and pyjamas. She is carrying a shopping bag.*

Moya   I thought I heard a noise.

Johnny   It's only us, Ma.

Moya   God, you're up late.

Johnny   We're only shooting the breeze.

Moya   Did anyone come, no?

Johnny *catches* **Medbh**'s *eye.*

Johnny   Yeah, yeah. A few people came by from the college. From the library I think. I went up to you but you were asleep.

Moya   God, Johnny, you should have woken me. What'll they think?

Johnny   They only stayed for a quick drink.

Moya   Still, though. I feel awful now. Who were they?

Johnny   I can't remember. A few dry shites in suits.

Moya   God. Was Professor Thompson here?

Johnny   I didn't catch the names.

Moya   I feel desperate now. What kind of tinker will they think I am?

Johnny   Well, don't feel desperate, Ma. They were fine. They understood. They only wanted to drop in.

Moya   Were you out, Medbh, love?

Medbh   No, Ma. I just ran down to Mairead for an hour.

Moya   Look at you both, drinking and smoking away. It's like a speakeasy in here. Where's the other two?

Medbh   They're in bed, I think.

Moya   They're not. I looked just now. And I wanted to apologise for losing the run of myself earlier. It's a terrible thing to let the sun go down on your anger.

Johnny   She had it coming, Ma.

Moya   I'm ashamed of myself now, I must say. I don't know what came over me. I don't feel very big.

Medbh   I don't know where they are.

Moya   I hope they're all right anyway. It's not much of a night to be walking the streets.

Medbh   I think I'll turn in anyway. I'm jacked. Good night, Ma.

Medbh *kisses her mother.*

Moya   Good night, pet. And thanks for all your help.

Medbh *kisses* **Johnny**.

Medbh   Good night, sweet prince.

Johnny   Yeah, yeah. Get thee to a fucking nunnery.

Medbh *leaves.*

Moya   It's so good to see you, love. You look well.

Johnny   I'm always well, Mother. You know that.

Moya   No you're not. Nobody's always well.

Johnny   Well, I am.

Moya *hands him the shopping bag.*

Moya   Look in that for me, love. I haven't my glasses. I'm
sorting them out for the library. Daddy's books. Just read me
out the names on them.

Johnny *takes out a handful of books and reads their titles.*

Johnny   There's a Collected Yeats, Heaney, Auden, Philip
Larkin . . .

Moya   They can have all those. Put them in the box.

Johnny *throws them into the tea chest, behind the sofa.*

Johnny   Milton, Marvell, Thomas Kinsella, Paul Durcan,
Derek Mahon, Sylvia Plath.

Moya   Those too.

He throws them into the chest and rummages again in the bag.

Johnny   What's this old one? *The Love Songs of Connaught*, by
Douglas Hyde.

Moya   That too.

Johnny   It looks old, Ma. It might be worth a few bob.

Moya   Not at all. Give it in to them where someone might
read it.

Johnny   It's too good for the library, Ma.

Moya   Indeed it's not. What's a book that no one reads?

Johnny   OK. If you're sure.

He throws it into the tea chest.

That's all.

They sit down together on the sofa.

Moya   Well, we'll have a good time, all of us together, now that you're over. And a bit of a chat. Sure, I hardly ever see you now that you're over there.

Johnny   Yeah. Look, I meant to tell you earlier, Ma. I'm going back tomorrow.

Moya   What?

Johnny   I've to go back to London tomorrow. First thing.

Moya   But you've only just got here, Johnny. Stop play-acting now. I mean you can't go back tomorrow when you've only just got here.

Johnny   There's some stuff I have to do.

Moya   What do you have to do? Would you not stay for a while?

Johnny   I'm going back.

Moya   Don't go, son. Please.

Johnny   It's Jenny. She's pregnant.

Moya   I'm sure she is. If this is another one of your spoofs.

Johnny   I wish it was. She is, Ma. She's three months gone.

Moya   Well. Isn't that great? Why didn't you tell me before?

Johnny   What's so great about it?

Moya   Well, I mean, if that's what you want. I mean, I don't understand. If that's what you want, that's wonderful news isn't it?

Johnny   It's not what I want. A mortgage and nappies and driving out to the country on a Sunday to see all the woollybacks. All that. I wanted her to get rid of it.

Moya   That's a big decision, Johnny.

Johnny   What's so big about it?

Moya   That's not an easy thing for any woman. You know that yourself. You know what Medbh went through.

Johnny   No. Well, she wants to keep it anyway. So that's what we're doing. We're keeping it.

Moya   Well, would you not stay here for a few days and think it over. Just relax for a few days.

Johnny   I'm going tomorrow, Ma. I'm going home.

Moya   Why are you going? If you don't want that life?

Johnny   You know why.

Moya   Why? Tell me?

Johnny   Because I wouldn't do what he did.

Moya   What do you mean?

Johnny   You know well what I mean.

Moya *laughs*.

Moya   Johnny. I'm sure I don't.

Johnny   Don't, Ma. He told me about it years ago.

Moya   What did he tell you? What?

Johnny   He told me about Helen.

Moya   What?

Johnny   Don't make me paint you a picture, Ma. I know you know.

Moya   I'm sure I don't.

Johnny   The girl your man Tom was talking about. The one with the birthmark on her face. In the church. You know well who she was.

Moya   He told you about it?

Johnny   He had to.

Moya   Why did he do that?

Johnny   I'm the executor of the will, Ma. He wanted to look after her. It's not much. There's the house, a bit of life insurance for you. A few bits and pieces. And there's just a small covenant in it for her. To pay off her college loan.

Moya   You're the executor?

Johnny   Yeah. Gas, isn't it?

Moya *is silent for a few moments.*

Moya   And he told you everything?

Johnny   Yeah. I think he just wanted to tell someone. It was after he had the bypass, you know. He said it was a terrible thing, having to live with a secret.

Moya   My God.

Johnny   Are you shocked?

Moya   I always meant to tell you about it, love. You of all of them. I thought you'd understand. Because he was so young. His head was turned. It was just after I lost the child, you see. There was a distance between us then, I don't know why. We weren't getting on and it was a thing that happened before we had a chance to settle down again. You shouldn't judge your father for that.

Johnny   I'm not judging him. That's more than he did for me.

Moya   And the girl got pregnant on purpose. She trapped him.

Johnny   Oh yeah. Sure she did.

Moya   There's a good word for what she was, Johnny, but I wouldn't use it. She was well known for it.

Johnny   She had a hard enough time, I believe. When dad left her by herself to have the kid.

Moya (*with sarcasm*)   I'm sure she did.

Johnny   Sure, you know she did. Didn't he tell you that?

Moya   Your father and me had more to talk about than that one, believe you me. She needn't think she'll see anything your father had anyway. She needn't think that for a minute.

Johnny   She's dead, Ma. She died a few years ago. Over in England.

Silence.

Moya   And I'm supposed to feel sorry, am I? She wanted to ruin everything. For me and your father, and for you and your two sisters. And she would have too if she'd been let.

Johnny   My three sisters, Ma. Remember your Chekhov. My three sisters. Helen's as much dad's daughter as Medbh or Catherine.

Moya   You needn't Helen me. She's no sister of yours.

Johnny   Ma, for God's sake.

Moya   She's nothing to this family and anyone who says she is needn't think they'll get the time of day from me.

Johnny   All right, Ma. Relax.

Moya   I loved Enda and he loved me. That was the way it was. We were married and that was the way it was.

Johnny   I know he loved you. He told me that.

Moya   Did he?

Johnny   Yeah. He did.

Moya   Did he really say that?

Johnny   Yes.

Moya   He stopped telling me that, you know. After we were married. He changed. I couldn't see it at first. But then he just stopped telling me he loved me. And I'd tell him all the time. I'd say it in the mornings when I woke up beside him. And he'd feel all warm and drowsy, you know, the way men do in the mornings. And I'd just say, Enda, I love you. Just that. And all he ever said to me was, I know you're fond of me anyway, for you put up with me. And if he'd just said it to me even sometimes, I would have been so . . . comforted. But he didn't. So then after a while I just stopped saying it to him too.

Johnny   Well, he never said it to me either.

Moya   He never even wrote me a love poem. Not even one of his silly bloody poems. It wouldn't have been much to ask, would it, son? For all those years.

Johnny   No. It wouldn't.

Moya   There was only once when he said . . . It was shortly after you were born. He was so happy when you came along, Johnny. After the two girls. There was a lightness about him then. There was an air of something . . . He came into the kitchen one morning with you in his arms, sleeping, and he said it in Irish. *A stóirín, ta grá agam dhuit.* Darling, I love you. I can see his face still. The time he said it in Irish. And we put you to sleep in the cot. And then we went upstairs and we made love.

Johnny   You've a great memory.

Moya   Well, I remember that day well. Because it was the last day we ever made love.

Johnny *takes her hand and squeezes it.*

Johnny   He didn't deserve you, Ma.

Moya   He deserved a lot better than me.

Johnny   They don't come any better than you and that's the truth.

Moya   And did she ever get married?

Johnny   Who?

Moya   That woman. Did she ever get married afterwards, do you know?

Johnny   Yeah. She did. She married some Scottish bloke, apparently. He worked in a bank. She was living over in Manchester. And then Helen found her a few years ago. Through the agency, you know. And that was how she found dad.

Moya   He never told me that. I mean, he told me she'd found him, of course. It brought it all up again. But nothing else.

Johnny   No. Well, I think he didn't want to hurt you.

Moya   And have you met her? The girl?

Johnny   No. I haven't. I've seen pictures, that's all.

Moya   Catherine and Medbh. Please don't ever tell them. What your father told you.

Johnny   Why not?

Moya   I don't know. Because I asked you not to?

Johnny   I wouldn't have anyway. Not now. They'd've rushed us off to family therapy or something. We'd all have been on the Oprah Winfrey show in the morning. Or Jerry Ryan on the fucking radio.

Moya   Oh, son, I get a laugh out of you anyway. I wish you'd stay for a while. Would you not?

Johnny   I can't.

Moya   Would you not ring Jenny and get her to come over?

Johnny   I said I'd go back to her.

Moya   Well, if you have to. But there'll always be a home for you here. You and anyone you want, love. You remember that.

Johnny   Yeah, well, I have to go. So there's nothing more to be said. So I'm going up to bed. I'm a poet, Ma, like himself.

Moya (*laughs*)   Sure, you can't, son.

Johnny   Why not?

Moya   There's only your father's bed free.

Johnny   That'll do.

Moya   You can't sleep in your father's bed.

Johnny   Why not?

Moya   It wouldn't be right.

Johnny   I'm not the sentimental type, Ma. You know that.

Johnny *goes towards the door.*

Moya   Johnny?

Johnny   What?

Moya   Nobody came, did they? From the pub.

Silence.

Johnny   They did, Ma. A few of them from the college. I didn't know who they were. They only stayed for a quick drink.

Moya   Really?

Johnny   Truly.

Moya   Well, I wish you'd woken me.

Johnny   Well, I should've. I'm sorry.

He goes towards the door again. He pauses in the doorway.

I love you, Ma. You know that, don't you?

Moya   Yes, son. I know that.

Johnny *leaves.* **Moya** *stands and begins clearing up plates of food. After a moment or two, she begins to cry. She drops the plates, holds her hands to her face and sobs violently, then tries to gather her*

*composure. She goes to the interior door. She takes a look at the room.
She turns off the lights and leaves the room, her body shaking with
tears. She closes the door behind her, and as she does so, the video
switches itself on. The screen shows* **Enda***'s face in tight close-up. He
stares at the camera for a moment, then begins to speak. It is obvious
from his declamatory style that he is speaking a poem.*

Enda
A Christmas Eve. I could not sleep
And so threw on some clothes and came in here
And sat dazed at the desk and tried to type
A word or two; and sensed an oddly rare
Nocturnal kind of pleasure, as outside
The midnight blackbirds gossiped in the yews.
Hard rain and storm relentless on the roads.
The ghosts of long gone dreams, the clacking of keys . . .

Enter **Catherine** *and* **Tom** *from the outer door. (Their clothing is
vague enough to also allow a suggestion of* **Young Moya** *and*
Young Enda*.) They ignore the video, smile at each other, steal
silently and slowly over to the sofa hand in hand. They lie down on the
sofa and embrace. They begin to kiss passionately.*

Enda
. . . And then I heard you cry out as you dreamed.
I stood, framed in the door, and gently called you.
Next, scared to cross the threshold, lest you stirred,
A century passed before I came and held you.
You said my name. I felt your body quiver.
Moya, love, you opened doors I thought I'd closed for
    ever.

And dreams? Were you asleep or was it me?
As I dithered, typing out redundant schemes,
All raw with you. Your lips. Your face aglow.
You, trailing sheets, chased through the ghostly rooms
And battled hard with men who wanted money.
Should I have been there, Moya, while you fought,
Instead of with my dreams? Well, clearly any
Man lost in the darkness will finally call it light.

And I had lost myself before I found you.
Yet in finding you I lost what I once had.
I have lost myself again. The light around you
Led me tearful from the darkness where I'd fled.
Your sleeping face, that love-filled sigh
Awakened something long asleep in me.

Thunder rolls. On the video screen, **Enda** *stands up. He walks towards the camera. He pauses for a moment, before looking closely into the lens. He laughs, gently. On the sofa,* **Tom** *and* **Catherine** *are still kissing.*

Enda   Ladies and gentlemen, Elvis has left the building.

He laughs again, winks, switches the camera off. White noise on the screen. Fade to darkness.